PRAISE FOR *PERMISSION TO SPEAK FREELY*

"This book is messy, like life. Anne has the insight, the guts, and the love to show us what has been in front of us all along, and to talk about the things we're afraid to talk about. It's a rare gift, one that she's willing to share."

SETH GODIN
Author, *Linchpin* and *Tribes*

"Anne Jackson tells the truth in such a way you can hear it. She is an objective journalist, and as such an endangered species. She's living proof that the truth, if stated clearly and objectively, can be fascinating."

DONALD MILLER
Author, *Blue Like Jazz* and *A Million Miles in a Thousand Years*

"Anne is disarmingly honest. She speaks the truth and allows us space to respond. She shines a light into the dark corners of our churches and our hearts and lets us know that it is safe to come out now into the freedom of God's grace. The writing of some books comes easily. I don't imagine for a moment that this one did, but the beauty contained within these pages will touch you deeply. I am grateful for the gift."

SHEILA WALSH
Author, *Beautiful Things Happen When A Woman Trusts God*

"Startling. Stunning. Fresh. Important. Relevant. Honest."

PATSY CLAIRMONT
Author, *Kaleidoscope: Seeing God's Wit and Wisdom in a Whole New Light*

"Folks don't expect Christians to be perfect. But they do expect us to be honest. Here is a fresh dream for a church where people can say 'I'm sorry' . . . and hear 'you are forgiven and loved.' It is a dream for a church where we can admit we are broken and be reminded that we are beloved. In these pages the Good News sounds good again, and you sense that Jesus really was sent not to condemn the world but to save it. Jackson doesn't excuse the hypocrisy of Christians, but she invites us to confront our hypocrisy and to make room for another hypocrite to be caught by grace."

SHANE CLAIBORNE
Author, Activist, and Recovering Sinner

"This is a huge risk of a book. But Anne Jackson has ventured on the tightrope and turned teetering into a tango. Jackson's is a fresh new voice, one already stylish, assured, distinctive, true."

LEONARD SWEET
Drew Theological School, George Fox University

"If you have ever struggled deeply in life and faith, and longed for someone who would understand, you must read this book. Anne's gripping narrative is authentic, real, and also provides a substantive hope in God and his healing process."

DR. JOHN TOWNSEND
Author of *Boundaries*
Psychologist, Speaker, Leadership Consultant

"The Bible says we're to confess our sins one to another and also tells us to carry each other when we're weak. Anne's latest book, *Permission To Speak Freely*, is a great read that clearly communicates these biblical principles in a captivating story. *Permission to Speak Freely* shows us that what's beautiful is oftentimes made up of very broken pieces."

CRAIG GROSS
Pastor, XXXchurch.com
Author, *Jesus Loves You This I Know* and *The Gutter*

"For years, Anne Jackson gave readers and writers permission to speak honestly on blogs. From topics no one talked about to confessions everyone pretended they didn't need to make, there was no subject Anne shied away from. Now, with this book, she's taking her raw, beautiful approach to honesty out of the blogs and into the place we need it most—the church. This is a mustard-seed book. Small, powerful, and bound to spread in ways I can't begin to understand."

JONATHAN ACUFF
Author, *Stuff Christians Like*

"Breaking down the walls surrounding faith, Anne weaves a current-day tapestry reminiscent of classics like *Pilgrim's Progress* or *Hinds Feet in High Places* that peek inside the broken human spirit while testifying to the beauty of second chances. She begs the reader to analyze their honest struggle between faith, fear, morality, and sacrifice. This book brings to light so many of the heartbreakingly raw confessions I've heard behind closed doors and is a great reminder that often the most ashamed become the most adept at embracing those who are running home from their failure."

TONY WOOD
Teaching Pastor, Crossroads Church, Corona, CA

"We have a sin problem in religious circles these days. The problem isn't that we sin (everyone has that problem) but that we can't talk about it. Anne's latest book gives people the permission to be real and honest about the struggles they have in life. In typical Anne Jackson fashion, she gives people the courage to drag their stuff from the darkness to the light. This is an important book for anyone who desperately needs freedom."

PETE WILSON
Author, *Plan B*

"Anne Jackson offers us a candid telling of her story—intimate and often painful, revelatory and saturated with humanity. Her encounters beckon us to embrace our brokenness, leading with confession and weakness, and in turn finding healing through those who have shared similar secrets and pain. She pushes against the undercurrent of the church culture that not-so-subtly implies that we must have it all together, bringing only our best before God and one another. Surely God desires for His children to receive grace and restoration through one another's stories, ultimately finding the things we need from Jesus in each other."

CHARLIE LOWELL
Jars of Clay

"There is a duality to the heart that is difficult to talk about. Anne Jackson sets us squarely in view of the best and worst of who we are. And in these pages she invites us to see that the gospel can handle the full weight of humanity in all its glorious conditions. There is freedom in these words."

DAN HASELTINE
Jars of Clay

"If the honesty, rawness, healthy questioning, and uncomfortable truthfulness that Anne writes about in this book would become normative, imagine what wonderful churches we would have and how Christianity would be rebirthed into something so biblically beautiful."

DAN KIMBALL
Author, *They Like Jesus But Not The Church*

"Brutally honest, beautifully written, and creatively imagined, *Permission to Speak Freely* is like ointment to a wound. Anne not only reminds us how painful the wound is, but she points to the healing we can experience in knowing we are not alone. Her authentic writing and unique perspective comes out powerfully on every page. This is a book I'll share with friends who need hope and encouragement."

JUD WILHITE
Author, *Eyes Wide Open*
Sr. Pastor, Central Christian Church, Las Vegas

"In a day where so many of us are quick with our answers, Anne is saying that the questions matter, and that perhaps we're loved by a God who can handle our questions, can handle our messes. And perhaps we're called to meet each other in these broken places. This book is an invitation to honesty and freedom, and to the possibility that we've been created to be truly loved and truly known."

JAMIE TWORKOWSKI
Founder, To Write Love on Her Arms.

"Anne Jackson is the real deal. And Anne is giving us all hope. Hope to be real, be authentic, and be the church. Hope to find healing. Hope that confession is cleansing. And ultimately hope in the promise that we are all being rescued. This book is a wake-up call for us all to quit trying to hide what's really going on, and instead find true community and live out the privilege we have to 'carry each other.' Read this book!"

BRAD LOMENICK
Director, Catalyst

"Anne's book is a gift to anyone who reads it. She opens the door to freedom and restoration by engaging readers in story, 'user-generated' art, and biblical truth. We're reminded that confession is the key—while making it clear: the church simply *must* be a safe place for this to happen."

NICK PURDY
Publisher, Paste Magazine

"Anne Jackson's *Permission to Speak Freely* is a refreshingly transparent invitation to explore our own human frailty and the paradoxical beauty of God's grace in the midst of our pain. Anne masterfully articulates her own journey and models the kind of honesty and generosity that will stir a renewal of hope in a new generation of wounded healers, about a God who really is present."

CHARLES LEE
CEO, Ideation Consultancy Inc.

"I'm going to be brutally honest. I don't *like* this book—not because it's not a worthwhile read but because it challenges me, makes me feel uncomfortable, and forces me to examine my inclination toward silence and projection. In short, it confronts many of the so-called elephants in the room—in our lives, faith, and our churches. Thankfully, there's good news, and this book reminds and invites us to a Grace that is so much greater than elephants."

EUGENE CHO
Pastor and Humanitarian

"The transparent and authentic life has just been reinvented. It will be absolutely impossible to be the same person when you are done with Anne's book. *Permission to Speak Freely* is devastatingly powerful and transforming. WOW!"

MIKE FOSTER
PlainJoe Studios and People of the Second Chance

"Through crowdsourcing and personal stories, Anne Jackson has crafted a masterpiece with honest conversation starters that every community must address."

JEFF SHINABARGER
Founder, Plywood People and *GiftCardGiver.com*

PERMISSION *to* SPEAK
FREELY

No. 05872

PERMISSION *to* SPEAK FREELY

Essays and Art
on Fear, Confession, and Grace

ANNE JACKSON

NASHVILLE DALLAS MEXICO CITY RIO DE JANEIRO

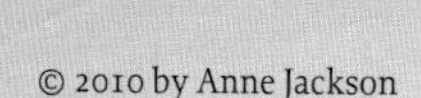

Published in Nashville, Tennessee, by Thomas Nelson. Thomas Nelson is a registered trademark of Thomas Nelson, Inc.

Thomas Nelson, Inc., titles may be purchased in bulk for educational, business, fund-raising, or sales promotional use. For information, please e-mail SpecialMarkets@ThomasNelson.com.

Some of the names of the people mentioned in this book have been changed to protect their privacy.

Library of Congress Cataloging-in-Publication Data

Jackson, Anne, 1980–
Permission to speak freely : essays and art on fear, confession, and grace / Anne Jackson.
p. cm.
ISBN 978-0-8499-4599-1 (pbk.)
1. Jackson, Anne, 1980– 2. Christian biography—United States. 3. Sexual abuse victims—United States—Biography. I. Title.
BR1725.J315A3 2010
248.8'6092—dc22
[B]
2010016658

Printed in China

13 14 15 16 RRD 9 8 7 6 5 4 3 2

To Mr. John David Bennett.
And to S and D,
with inexpressible gratitude
for teaching and inspiring.

CONTENTS

INTRODUCTION

In May 2008, I asked a question on my blog, FlowerDust.net.

What is one thing you feel you can't say in the church?

Hundreds of people responded. The question spread far—both in the Christian faith and outside, even being posted and discussed on a highly regarded atheist blog. The conversation went global. Websites in the UK and a radio station in Australia took the question and posed it to their own audiences. Regardless of someone's religion (or lack thereof), it appeared that everyone had input.

Those outside the Christian faith spoke familiar sentiments

about the facade the evangelical movement has created over the centuries.

- "Christians say one thing and do another."
- "If Christians can't be who they are within their own churches, why are they even a part of church? Why not go someplace where they can be themselves?"

We've all heard those accusations. From the media, to people in our workplaces, to our families, this perception comes as no surprise.

As far as those within the Christian faith, the responses to the question were as intriguing as they were heartbreaking.

- "I currently feel no connection to God when I pray or read the Bible."
- "I have been a Christian for 27 years and I still don't understand the point of praying."
- "Sometimes I wonder if this whole Christianity thing is a lie."
- "Most of the time I never feel forgiven for my sins . . . partly because it's hard to forgive myself . . . the other part is that church people seem to never let you let it go and move forward."
- "I'm a pacifist."
- "Why do we have lavish worship centers but there are starving children in our own backyards and around the world?"

Some boldly placed their names, even links to their websites or blogs, while others remained apprehensively in the shadow, concerned that even the modest anonymity the Internet offered was not enough to protect them from being judged.

Of course, the root of the question didn't stem completely from social curiosity. It came from places in my own heart and life where I was afraid to say something inside a church or to other Christians. Fear had kept me silent, had overruled confession, and I needed to know I wasn't alone.

So I asked the question.

And the responses continue coming.

People have shared thoughts about politics and sex and mental illness and abuse and confusion and racism and Jesus and poverty and music and addictions and money. They all felt, for some reason, they couldn't freely discuss these topics (and many others) in the church.

A year and a half later, the website PermissionToSpeakFreely.com launched, asking for artistic submissions of confessions (photos, postcards, letters, anything really) to be used in this book and on the website.

What are people afraid of? What's holding them back? How do faith and brokenness coexist? Why do bad things happen? Where is God in all of the mess?

The purpose of this book is simple: to share the confessions I've received from the website or through the mail, as well as stories from my own life and experience, to show you that you're not alone in your battle with fear and secrets. I know not everyone who thumbs through the pages of this book is a Christian. I am, and so I write this from an ever-exploring, continually learning, faith-based point of view.

I believe there is a force rooted in evil and fear, and it has latched onto us. As you'll see, the things people have said about the church and about other Christians are painful, even bitter sometimes. I know the things I've said about the church have been hateful too. What people feel they can't say in church is often heartbreaking.

To be frank, I am somewhat tentative to share some of these confessions and stories because I don't want to paint a negative picture of the magnificent creation of the church. So with that said, please know the confessions that are shared aren't directed *at* the church.

Instead, I believe the confessions in this book fly as misdirected arrows, coming from hearts so wounded they desperately need grace, freedom, clarity, beauty . . .

. . . and hope.

I pray as we all read these confessions together, and eventually share some of our own, that we will feel comforted that we are not isolated in our brokenness.

I pray that we will be unified more by our common humanity and need for divine intervention, and that we'll be separated less by darkness and loneliness.

But more than that, I hope we realize we're not alone in a Savior's plan to rescue us.

While I have your attention and am explaining some

things in advance, I should help you shape your expectation now. This book isn't a how-to book chock-full of practical advice and step-by-step instructions that will guarantee your freedom from every one of your secrets or every ounce of your shame.

It's my opinion that many times we have been given easy answers that may temporarily act as good advice, but we aren't cookie-cutter humans, and those easy answers won't satisfy a story that's eternal. A formula will not work in the long run. Sometimes a formula won't work at all. Discovering why we feel trapped by fear or shame, and how God wants to begin to heal our brokenness, is a personal journey that nobody on the face of this earth has the right to define or say how it should look in order for it to be true.

Your journey is providentially crafted for you.

What I consider this book to be is a layering of my own stories of battling fear, hiding from God, hating the church, loving the church, and finding myself on a never-ending quest for more truth and more grace. Throughout the book, you'll find confessions that other people have sent to me. There are also some beautifully composed lyrics and a smattering of poetry, art, and Scripture. And if you go to the website PermissionToSpeakFreely.com, you'll find even more confessions, essays, and poetry, since this expedition to find courage and permission doesn't end when you close this book.

As you go through these pages, I hope you'll see the transformative power of grace and mercy that each story contains—whether it is my own or somebody else's. And through these stories, I hope you will understand the same remarkable grace is everywhere and ready to capture you.

SOMETIMES I FEEL LIKE A LAMP THAT'S BURNED OUT.

KATIE MAY LOOK PRETTY ON THE OUTSIDE BUT INSIDE KATIE IS DEAD. KATIE IS TIRED. KATIE IS WEAK. SOMETIMES, KATIE DOESN'T WANT TO DO IT ANYMORE. KATIE IS TIRED OF FIGHTING HER PHYSICAL BATTLES. SHE JUST WANTS TO BE HEALTHY. SHE WANTS TO FEEL GOOD. SHE DOESN'T.

SOMETIMES, THIS MAKES ME MAD AT GOD.

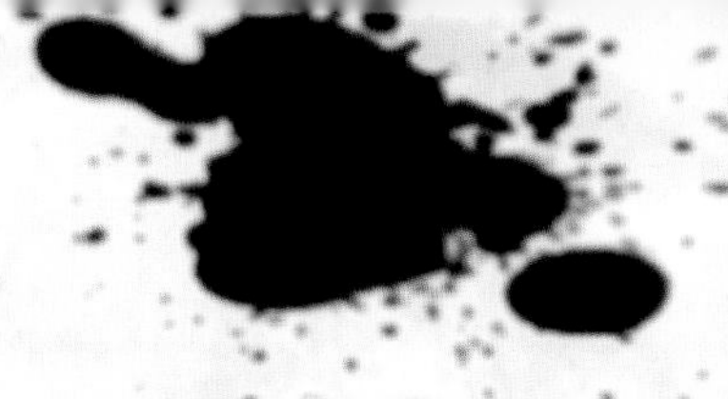

Everything is A-OK. Hunky dory. Grade A. A

I love everybody at my church. Equally. I am hap

My pastors are amazing, anointed people.

We ... speak in Christian-ese and our services

a... erstand for even the first-time

... Hunky dory. Gra

... am hap

Duct tape doesn't fix everything.

mary

We never ... es

are easy to underst... e

visitor. Everything is A-OK. ... Gra

I love everybody at my church. Equally. I am happ

My pastors are amazing, anointed people.

We never speak in C... and our services

are easy to unde... he first-time

visitor. Ever... dory. Gra

I love e...

We do what we

... do out of routine

... and perceived requirement. We do what

After my divorce, nobody called me.
It broke my heart. Again.

Mark.

Sometimes I'm afraid to
trust God because I'm afraid
of what He might have
in store for me.

— Travis

I can't believe
God was there when
I was sexually abused...

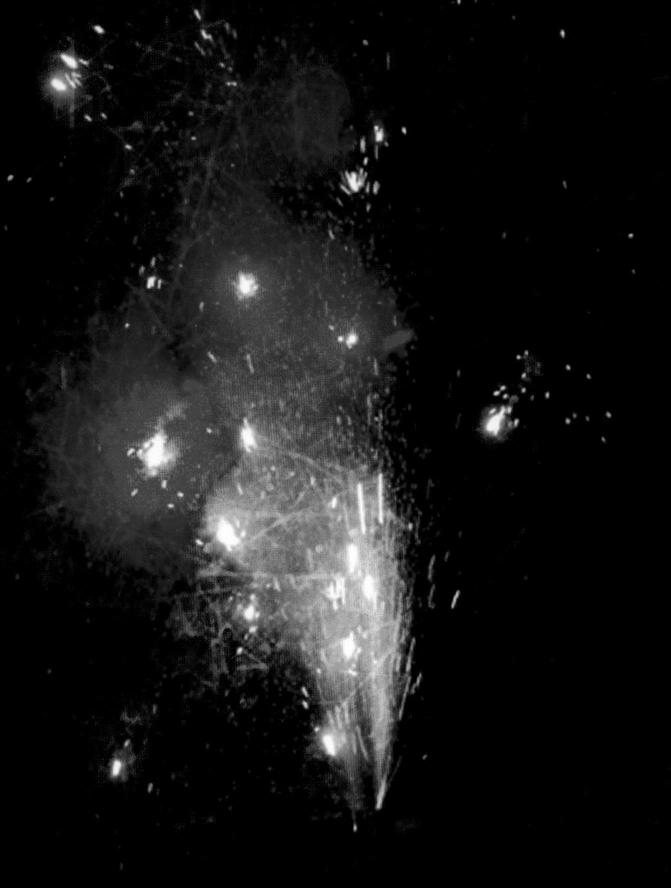

Jessica

Life still feels like it's exploding...

I've tried so hard
not to be the stereotypical Christian
that I've sinned against God.

Prudence

I placed every hard-earned quarter I received
in allowance into dated offering envelopes
because the adults at catechism classes
told me that their god wouldn't love me otherwise.

Is extorting money from
and manipulating children
the best way to teach generosity?

~ Heather

Over the years I've attended many churches – good ones. Most of them were small enough that we knew everyone else. We've had times when we couldn't go to church for more than a year because of sickness. And though I loved those churches, it bothers me that only once has anyone from any of them ever called to say "What's happening? We missed you. How are you?"

Didn't Jesus say "I was sick, and you visited me?" When we know people are sick, why don't we take more initiative to stay in touch and see how they are? Isn't it important to let people know we love them – and, through that, to assure them that God does too?

Pete

I am not who you perceive me to be –

Laila

Lord, I'm sorry for selfishly carrying out my own agenda rather than allowing Yours to sink into my soul.

– Dana

You're important to the work God is doing.

"The body is a unit,

though it is made up

of many parts...

So it is with Christ."

1 CORINTHIANS 12:12 NIV

I DON'T REALLY ENJOY BEING A PASTOR'S WIFE.

joanie

Part One

GHOSTS IN CATHEDRALS

Tension

tension
for a rope to have tension,
two forces must be pulling
as fiercely as possible
in opposite directions
yet called out
trying to balance
and understand
unity
freedom
humility
kingdom [1]

1

MEET FEAR

Fear has always been the antagonist in my life, and most of the time, I welcomed him. Ironically, he felt safe enough, and I would allow him to tag along as I walked through my day. I guess I'd liken him in some regard to my little brother, always following one step behind and occasionally running ahead of me.

Sometimes he annoyed me a bit, getting in the way when I needed him to leave me alone. In other instances, he'd embarrass me at the least opportune times. I couldn't always hide him, and it was obvious to everyone around that Fear was with me.

In my weakest moments, I'd let his presence overshadow me. A moment in time would pass when I knew I should say something, do something, offer something, or be something to someone—but with his strong arms wrapped around my own will, I gave in to Fear too easily.

Not even putting up a fight.

Fear won.

After three decades of letting Fear intimidate me, I've decided enough is enough. It's time to fight back. Fear may still exist and hide in the corners of my heart and my mind, but I refuse to allow him to have the control he once had.

Well, at least I'm attempting to try.

I realize Fear isn't only affecting me, but humanity as well. As I look around today, I see him hooking into many people I encounter. Their hearts are fighting for their dreams, yet Fear claws away at their spirits, telling them their dreams are impossible.

These people want to have a family, go back to school, quit their jobs and move to Africa, ask that girl out, volunteer at a shelter, stand up for justice, pose a question, right a wrong, or say hi to their neighbor, but Fear soaks into their bloodstream like a paralyzing virus and prevents them from taking a step in the beautiful, wonderful, difficult life in front of them.

Fear wants to stop our stories.

And with the pain and brokenness and hurt in this world, we simply can't let it. The human race needs a hope and faith and light now more than ever.

The Scriptures say that through the love of Christ, we are to be that hope. That light burning brightly on a hill. Not hidden in the darkness of a shadow of a nemesis named Fear.

Yet we can't fight it by ourselves.

I think that's why so many of us get so close to crossing over the line . . .

From darkness into light.

From Fear into boldness.

But we know that once we take that step into that which illuminates, we'll be exposed.

Naked.

Ashamed.

Broken.

Possibly alone, and desperately longing to go into hiding again.

And so we stay . . .

Silent.

We know what it's like to have Fear screaming in our heads.

Our minds tell us to run, tell us we're not good enough. Our hearts palpitate, our hands sweat, and our voices tremble.

Fear's voice is loud.

Earth-shatteringly loud.

But our voices are louder.

Yet most of us don't believe that.

We don't know the power we have when we fight back Fear. Fear isn't strong. He's derived from something ultimately weak and powerless.

Have you noticed how we're often impressed by people who appear to be fearless? The ones who fly to the moon. Chase tornadoes. Enter dangerous war zones. Skydive. Speak in front of thousands of people. Stand up to cancer. Raise money and adopt a child who isn't their flesh and blood.

Why are we so inspired by them?

Because deep down, *we are them.*

We all share those characteristics. They're divinely human.

Just like us.

Something in us begins to come alive when we see people overcome Fear. Their actions push us to find that divine piece (or is it peace?) within ourselves so that we may also overcome Fear.

We wrestle for a while and get frustrated that, in the end, we've lost the battle again (and again and again). So we retreat back into ourselves, hiding our secrets and our questions under a cloak of safe normalcy and commonality.

Yet the only thing that's normal and common about us is that we all have our issues. Each of us.

We all have . . .

A shame.

A weight.

A burden.

A question.

A past.

Fear continues to tell us that, because of these secrets, we're alone.

And that we can't speak freely.

But Fear is wrong.

We are not alone.

Regardless of what shame, what question, what trepidation, what history, what anxiety, whatever you are carrying deep inside, you are not alone.

Scripture says we have not been given a spirit of fear.

So why do so many of us experience Fear?

Why do so many of us continue to feel trapped?

And why, of all the places on earth, do we fear revealing our secrets in the church?

2

CHURCH CLOTHES

Much of our current reality is shaped by our past. This is exceedingly true in regard to our cultural viewpoint. My own history of growing up in the church, the daughter of a preacher man, tints the lens through which I view faith and life.

We lived in a suburb of Fort Worth, Texas. I was three years old, give or take, and I remember my mother dressing me in some kind of blue jumper dress, red tights, and these unforgivably stiff, patent dress shoes.

These were my church clothes. My Sunday best. Anything

less wouldn't pass the approval of God. Or at the very least, my Sunday school teachers.

I'd carry my white New Testament (the full Bible was too heavy for me), and off we'd go to our Very Traditional Southern Baptist Church. My parents would hand over my screaming baby brother to kind, blue-haired women in the nursery and then take me down to children's church, stopping along the way so they could chat with other parents. I'd coyly bury my face in the back of my dad's navy polyester trousers, at times peeking at all the kneecaps and purses around me.

As the bell rang, signaling the start time for Sunday school, the adults' conversations would end and my parents would whisk me off down a long, threadbare, blue-carpeted hallway toward the classroom for three-year-olds.

There were maybe fifteen or so other kids in my class, mostly boys who had Cheerio dust on their button-up shirts and an affinity for playing with their private parts. I remember learning a few songs about becoming a soldier in the Lord's Army, that the word *butt* was a bad word, and that you couldn't die from swallowing soap, since the little boy who said "butt" came back the following Sunday after having his mouth washed out from saying it.

It was at this time in my life when the smell of an old Baptist church became permanently burned into my nose and into my memory. I don't know how they did it, but every Baptist church built between 1940 and 1980 carries the same scent of oak pews, hymnal pages, and musty paint.

A couple of years later, my dad became the pastor of his own Very Traditional Southern Baptist Church. I was five years old, and the church our family was called to was the only church in the small farming panhandle town of Circle Back, Texas. Aside from some tumbleweeds and cattle, our family made up the entire population of Circle Back.

But you can't have a church without people. The equally odd-named communities around Circle Back (like Muleshoe and Needmore) didn't have churches, so that's where the twenty or so families who attended Circle Back Baptist would come from. One guy would ride his tractor from his house, across a field, to the church every Sunday.

I'm not sure where the tradition began, whether it dates back to the Reformation or is perhaps something pastors are taught in seminary, but evidently when you are an immediate family member of the preacher, you must sit on the second pew of the church. It's the only place our family could sit. When I tried to sit with a friend, my mom would quickly pull me back to the second row as members of the congregation would whisper to one another and point at us from behind their hymnbooks.

A year or so later, my dad became a preacher at another Very Traditional Southern Baptist Church in another small town where we sat on another second row. And then another. And then another.

More dresses.

More patent dress shoes.

And more brushstrokes for the picture that I was learning to paint: I had to impress God by impressing God's people.

Being a bit rebellious in nature, as many pastors' children are, I fought this ideology. When I was in the second grade, after church one Sunday evening, a boy who was a few years older than I was started making fun of me. I chased him through the sanctuary and out the front door. I ran in the church, and I knew that was against the rules. It was a sin of moral consequence.

There were five really wide concrete stairs outside the front door of the church, which he leaped over with pubescent athletic elegance.

Me?

Not so much.

My right ankle folded under me, and I tumbled down the stairs to the sidewalk below.

Rushing to my side, my mother first made sure I was okay, then took me back to the church's kitchen to put ice on my ankle. A wake of deacons' wives hovered suspiciously in the doorway of the kitchen, commenting on how if my mother wouldn't have let me run inside the church, I wouldn't have been hurt to begin with.

"It's not that she was only running in church," one woman commented under her breath. "She was chasing *a boy*. You know God wouldn't allow that in His sanctuary."

So running in the church was punishable by bodily harm. Noted.

Over the next few years, not much changed. Jesus was distinguished as a gentle white man who obviously was a fan of Pantene (how else could His hair be so soft and shiny in the pictures?), and His Father, God, was the Angry General who kept us all in line because Jesus was too polite to do so. Jesus could tell us great stories, but it was God who had the final word.

The people in the churches we would attend, for the most part, played the role of God's mouthpiece, letting me know what He didn't like me to do. Like run in the church or wear jeans or sit somewhere other than the second row with my mom.

I searched the Bible for guidance and confirmation about where I was supposed to sit as a preacher's kid or what I was supposed to wear at church, but I couldn't find it anywhere.

The deacons' wives assured me it was in there somewhere and then flocked to find the next person who was clearly deserving of God's wrath.

What God said in the Bible, sometimes through Jesus, and what God said through the words of the deacons' wives was a contradiction.

Love? Peace? Joy? Anger? Pride? Unhappiness? The heart? Keeping up with appearances?

I began to wonder who, if anyone, I could trust.

And more importantly, I wondered if I'd ever be able to wear jeans in church like all the other kids my age did.

trust is not a four-letter word

trust is not a four-letter word.
[at least, that is what i keep reminding myself]

i think you know the place of which i speak.
the small area
[approximately the size of a quarter, i'd imagine]
which rests in the center of your chest:
between the cages of your ribs
beneath the muscles and tissues
of your heart and of your lungs

this is the place we feel trust
[or lack thereof]

at its most intense times
[when betrayal is fresh]
the pain and discomfort
radiate across our entire being

the tension in the neck
the pressure on your stomach
nauseated
[imagine the tire of a texas-sized truck
running over your torso
repeatedly; repeatedly]

arms folded
trying to protect the emotional;
the spiritual;
the mental;
using physical means
survival.

[*logical redemption*]

with grace
and time
forgiveness chosen
the once overwhelming
sensation of suffocation
retreats back into
aforementioned quarter-sized area
and quietly refrains
from causing disturbances
emerging and unsuspecting

hibernation
by definition
conserves energy in
those frigid winter months

but once the warmth of the sun
touches the air

[touches my being]
instead of spring
the fear of feeling
those things that have been
felt before
[crushing me before]
[shredding me before]
emerge

questioning this new light
[or this one? or this one?]
is real; shining; radiating?

perhaps another fluorescent clone
which will project
a washing out of my skin
[grey]
[lifeless?]

i find myself
staying . . .
. . . buried

still afraid
and unable to find it.

[to find trust][2]

3

THE FIRST BRICK

We all remember the first time we had our faith in someone betrayed. The moment when innocence began morphing into skepticism.

Mine happened on a playground in the fourth grade.

I found myself dusting the gritty hot sand off my hands and knees as my supposed best friends stood laughing at me. Leigh and Amy. Daughters of deacons at the church where my dad was the pastor.

As a welcoming gift a few weeks earlier, they offered me the middle part of a three-piece heart necklace. You know the kind. The type that reads "Best Friends Forever" when the parts are put together.

I considered it part of my own heart. And in a way, it was. Finally, something stable. Something promising. Something consistent in my inconsistent life. This new school was the third school I had attended since kindergarten because we moved around so much.

I believed maybe this time, these friendships would be different. They'd be forever, just like the pendant said.

But after school one day, Amy reached out and tore the necklace off my suntanned neck. Leigh pushed me down into the sand under a plastic green slide.

"We never wanted to be your best friend! Our parents made us!"

I stared at them, holding back my tears and feeling one of the chambers of my heart twist. It felt strange, and it hurt. Until that minute in my ten years on earth, I had never felt that before.

Clenching my teeth and ignoring the pain from the scrapes on my knees and my twisted-up heart, I did what any ten-year-old would do.

I ran.

Home.

We only lived about a quarter of a mile from the playground. My scrawny legs carried me faster than I had ever run before. I tore into the house, the storm door slamming behind me. I continued running down the hall until I reached my bedroom, where I threw my sandy, sweaty, heaving body on the bed. Burying my face in my favorite pink-flowered pillowcase, I sobbed.

I sobbed and I sobbed and I sobbed.

My mother, concerned about the unusual commotion from her typically quiet daughter, sat down gently at the foot of my bed. She waited a few minutes until my weeping subsided and asked what had happened.

In between gulps and hiccups and wiping generous amounts of mucus from my face, I told her that Leigh and Amy hated me. That I hated moving and I missed my old friends and I hated deacons and school and my life and I hated the church.

My mom quietly stroked my sweaty hair.

I now think she was quiet because she kind of agreed with me.

4

THE FINAL BRICK

As I got older, the disconnect between what I'd read in the Bible and what people in the church would actually say or do became more apparent and more confusing.

If there was anything being a Very Traditional Southern Baptist taught me, it was that I needed to know my Bible.

I think that if those really mean, really political people in the church really knew the power the words of the Bible held, they wouldn't want us reading it and memorizing it so much in Sunday school.

Themes of grace, forgiveness, and love are woven in and

ut of the tissue-thin pages. But proof of the opposite is more an often what so many of us experienced if we've spent any amount of time in church or around church people.

When I was sixteen, my family was at the last church my dad would ever pastor. It was in the booming town of Abilene, Texas. We had lived there around three—maybe four—years, and the inevitable mess of real life began to take its toll. People began to show who they really were, complaining about this or demanding that, and justifying their actions with "for the Bible tells me so," or "My daddy laid the foundation of this church," the latter statement carrying more weight than the former.

My dad, who was the senior pastor at this church, was passionate about caring for people who were far from faith. Because he believed everyone in the church should participate in helping others, he taught classes coaching people on why we should be concerned for our community and how to love people when they are going through a difficult time.

However, most people at this particular church had been members for life. Nobody had ever asked them to step out of their pews before. To them, you went to church three times a week, and that was how you found Jesus and built your mansion up in heaven. My dad was the one getting paid to care for people. Why in the world would he ask them to do the same without getting paid for it?

His challenging the status quo did not sit well with some of the congregation. After a few months of tension and secret meetings, my dad was asked to resign his position at one of the church's monthly business meetings.

And they didn't ask kindly either.

An avalanche of insults and lies tumbled down on my family and on another pastor in the church who supported my dad.

Things got ugly.

My mom started to cry.

People started yelling.

Filled with teenage impulsivity, I stood up.

(From the second pew, of course.)

I was done not saying things in church.

Flipping my Bible to Ephesians, I started reading about the unity of the church and how we needed to do everything to preserve it. How dare these people call themselves followers of Christ when all they did was fight and hate and lie? Still out to prove my point, I quickly thumbed to John 13 (see, all those Bible studies did come in handy) and said that the world is supposed to know we're followers of Christ by the love we have for each other. What if someone who wasn't a Christian had been sitting in the meeting? How would that person see Christ?

I could feel my heart pounding in my chest. And in my ears. And in my throat. And feet. I realized what I had just done and felt a little dizzy.

Being a teenage girl and trying to preach (sorry, *teach)* unity to a Very Traditional Southern Baptist Church as they're in the middle of splitting isn't the best way to have a message received. The rage the church members were projecting floated across the sanctuary to the second row and burned up my face. I turned Bloody Mary–mix red, a combination of anger and embarrassment.

Nobody said a word, but it was crystal clear I needed to leave.

After regaining the feeling in my legs, I stormed out, slamming the heavy wooden door behind me. That night, I felt like not only had people abandoned us, but we had been abandoned by God. I wrote a letter to Him, addressing Him as "Nobody," about the faith I was about to leave behind.

Another brick had been placed in the wall I had been building around my heart in an attempt to protect it from the damaging battles that raged in the church.

And this brick was the final one.

My dad resigned as pastor of that church at that meeting, and both he and my mom began searching for jobs. Whoever got the best job first would determine our family's future.

More than likely, we'd be moving.

Again.

5

LOSING FAITH

My dad "resigned" in April of my sophomore year. Months went by, the summer passed, and I thought maybe, just maybe, we'd end up staying in Abilene. After all, this was the longest we had lived anywhere. I began my junior year, was doing great academically, and had started playing basketball again after hurting my knee the year before. The only two people I trusted in the world were there—my best friend, Julie, and the object of my first starry-eyed romance, a senior named Nathan, who worked at IHOP and made the most amazing cherry cokes for me.

A month or two into my junior year, my mom got a job offer to teach at an elementary school in Dallas.

It was time to move.

Leaving Abilene meant leaving Julie and Nathan. And leaving Julie and Nathan meant leaving a hole in my heart bigger than the state of Texas.

The first sixteen years of my existence had included church, farming, basketball, and more church. Before moving to Dallas, Abilene was the largest city I'd lived in, and with three Christian colleges and a church on every corner, it was just about as full of Churchianity as a place could get.

Dallas was different.

Sure, there was still a church on every corner, but on the highways were strip clubs, big malls, and more billboards per square mile than I'd ever seen in my days living in West Texas. There were more than four radio stations, and many of them used words I had never heard before.

My dad was markedly depressed and withdrawn, and our family was pretty much financially ruined. When I enrolled in school, I learned that since I had been on an honors track my first two years of high school, I had more credits than a typical junior.

My school counselor informed me that if I dropped out of the honors program and stuck to the regular track, I could graduate as a junior that year. And if I graduated as a junior, that meant I could move out and move back to Abilene, back to Nathan (and Julie, too, of course). If all went as planned,

I would graduate a couple of months after my seventeenth birthday.

This new high school was enormous: well over five hundred kids in my grade and over two thousand on campus. And it was certainly more diverse than Abilene. Girls in the orchestra would make out in the bathrooms, and there were boys who wore makeup and had various body parts pierced.

We didn't go to church anywhere. We tried a few times, but it was too painful—for my dad, because he saw someone else in the pulpit living out his dream, and for my mom, because she projected her heartbreak and lack of trust on the members of whatever church we visited.

Even though I had officially told God I wanted nothing to do with Him, the culture shock of my new territory drove me to find comfortable space. I got a job working at a Christian bookstore down the road (aside from seminary students, there's nobody more knowledgeable about Bibles and Christian products than a lifelong preacher's kid).

At the bookstore, we got a poster to hang in our window for that year's "See You at the Pole," an annual event where students gather around their school's flagpole and pray. At my school in Abilene, I was one of the leaders every year. I wondered if my new school was participating, because I hadn't seen anything about it.

I checked around and found out that nobody had ever conducted a "See You at the Pole" at my new school. After making some calls to some churches and sending e-mails to some pastors, I tracked down a local youth minister who said he had some material I could use to start it up and advertise it.

Because we didn't go to church anywhere and he wasn't my youth pastor, we arranged to meet at a local Wal-Mart so he could hand off the posters and leader's kit. My mom drove me to the store, and I waited for him in the food court. He showed up, looking barely old enough to be called a pastor, wearing a ball cap. We sat down to go over the material.

It was going to be difficult to get momentum going because the event was only two weeks away, but I tried my best. Nervous that nobody would show up and I'd look like an idiot rocking out to the latest DC Talk album and praying by a flag-pole alone, when the morning of the prayer time approached, I stood off to the side to see if anyone even came close.

Nobody did.

So I went on to English class, once again certain that my decision to leave my faith behind was a good one.

A couple of days later, the youth pastor called to see how things went.

And then he asked me over to his place to watch a movie.

6

FINDING LOVE (IN ALL THE WRONG PLACES)

Most teenagers believe they're more mature than they really are. I know I did. So when this youth pastor in his midtwenties asked me over to see a movie, I didn't think twice about it. In fact, I was flattered that an older guy was interested in me, an all-grown-up sixteen-year-old girl. And he was a youth pastor. Maybe he could help me rediscover my faith. Part of me missed it.

Something I never had growing up was a curfew. My parents trusted me enough not to worry about where I was or who I was with. The two unspoken rules I had to live by were "Don't get put in Juvie" and "Don't get pregnant." As long as they never got a call from the police or the hospital, I was pretty much free to do whatever I wanted.

A basic "to a friend's house to watch a movie" appeased my parents as I walked out the door. Taking my mom's car to his apartment, I was more worried about driving in the Dallas traffic than I was about watching a movie with him.

I knocked on the door to his apartment, and he let me in. From the beginning, even as naive as I was, it was obvious what was on his mind. The lights were dimmed, and blankets and pillows were laid out on the floor to make the movie watching more . . . *comfortable.*

The details of that night aren't relevant, but it's safe to say I don't remember what movie we watched. The one thing I do remember is that as scary as this new experience was, a huge void in my heart had been filled, and for the first time in several months, I felt loved and accepted and worthy.

And I felt beautiful.

The youth pastor and I dated for a couple of months, and then he quietly slipped away. I was upset but decided to move on. The wounds on my heart caused by the pain from uprooting had started to open up again. I felt lonely, and I needed to find someone else to make the pain go away.

I went on a few dates with a couple of guys, but my heart still longed for this youth pastor. I'd given him so much of myself; how could it not?

After the holidays, the youth pastor called me, and we started dating again. He had moved to another part of Dallas and had a roommate now, so we'd meet in a park close to his new house. A few more months went by, and I had fallen back in love, head over heels.

Just before I graduated high school, while we were out one afternoon, he told me he was getting married. He had proposed to someone he knew from his past and said he could never see me again.

The youth pastor and this other woman had been dating via a long-distance relationship the entire time he and I had been seeing each other. She didn't know about me. And from the way I couldn't catch my breath and started seeing double, it was obvious that I didn't know about her either.

My heart broke. I was so naive and lonely that I actually had believed he loved me.

And he was a pastor. How could he have lied to me?

Oh, right, the logical side of my brain told me. *It's because he is a pastor.*

This experience became another piece of evidence that people who say they're close to God can't be trusted. And as far as I was concerned, God couldn't be trusted either.

There was a sharp pain in my chest where my heart once lived. It hurt so badly that my mind would scream at my heart and tell it to stop.

Will you ever stop hurting? I can't take it anymore.

I had to do something to medicate this pain. I had to escape it as if life itself depended on it.

And so I ran.

Again.

What's Done Is Done

Done
Foolish heart,
Wildest of dreams—
Things are never
Quite what they seem.
Innocent eyes,
Purest of minds
She's looking for something
That she'll never find.
Trusting in so much,
That's not worth trusting in
The person she's now
Meets who she could've been.
There are two roads to travel
She chose the wrong one
Now there's no going back
What's done is done.[3]

7

SHATTERED PIXELS

As you saw from my playground experience earlier, I run when hurt hunts me down. I put the blame for the pain I was experiencing from the "relationship" with this youth pastor on God and began to run from my faith again. God and I were through. He obviously didn't care about me, so I didn't care about Him anymore either.

To help numb the pain, I began experimenting with a lot of things that weren't healthy for me.

A little alcohol.

Some pills.

And pornography.

I know, I know. Porn is a guy's problem. Girls—especially teenage girls—don't look at porn.

And the last place you would expect to see porn is the living room of a former pastor, right?

But during these "dark years," between a portrait of my family taken at Christmastime and an old, broken, dot matrix printer sat a computer screen. The place where I typed book reports and instant-messaged my friends became the doorway to an endless amount of forbidden fruit—and even more amounts of guilt.

Still in culture shock from our move to Dallas, and now with an awakened sense of myself sexually, I began to notice the provocatively lit neon signs loudly proclaiming XXX and FULL NUDITY. On the way home from school on my bus, I overheard two boys talking about looking up images of people having sex online. Ignited teenage hormones combined with the new technology of the Internet proved to be a dangerous combination.

Late one night, after my parents and younger brother had gone to bed, I logged on and did an online search for "sex." I had no idea that typing that one word into a computer would lead me to an addiction I'd fight for years.

And it wasn't just a physical addiction either. Viewing these outwardly flawless women fed the huge emotional need that was left by my dad's withdrawal and the youth pastor's rejection. Through the fantasies I would have by looking at that computer screen, I would find love and affirmation.

I graduated as planned my junior year and moved out a few months after my seventeenth birthday. Now I had my own apartment with my own computer, and all the freedom in the world. I would go to work (now the manager of the Christian bookstore), come home, and look at porn almost every night. Soon my porn binges started affecting my performance at work and my relationships because I wouldn't get any sleep, and when I was with friends, I would secretly obsess about how soon I could be home and when I could get my next fix.

What's a girl to do?

Of course, I never mentioned my struggle to anyone. Looking at porn was typical, even expected, for men—but a girl? A girl who likes porn? I often questioned my sexual orientation. If I was straight, why did I like looking at naked women? So was I gay? Or bisexual? Or was I just perverted?

I hated the pattern I had fallen into. I think I knew it was wrong. At least I realized anything that caused this much obsession couldn't be right.

But I couldn't stop.

The addiction went from online to offline. When something as dark and lonely and shameful as a sexually oriented addiction has a grasp on you, you do a lot of things you'd never in a million, billion years dream you'd ever do.

My boundaries crumbled, and I began sexually experimenting, at times with men I barely knew. One night when I was almost eighteen, I remember going to a cute guy's house. He was a junior in college, and I had met him only a few days before at a local Waffle House. Aside from a few mental snapshots, I don't remember anything from that night except having a drink and waking up fuzzy, alone, half dressed on his couch. He was nowhere to be found; I dressed and went home. I never saw him or heard from him again.

I don't even remember his name.

By the time I was twenty, I settled down a little bit and was engaged to someone I had been dating for a while. But during the months leading up to the wedding, my old habits came back with a vengeance, and I began seeing another man behind my fiancé's back—and I got caught. After the wedding was called off, I rebounded by becoming a serial dater. I always needed to have a man in my life in order to feel worthy.

According to everything I had seen, to be accepted and loved meant to have a sexual relationship, and what girl doesn't need to be accepted and loved?

For years this addiction held me tightly in a dark embrace, and somewhere inside me I knew it wasn't the life I was intended to have. I knew it was wrong. And as I got older and began to rediscover my faith and my purpose and identity in Christ, I knew I had to break away from the safety I found in my morphed perspective of sex.

As twisted as it was, it was familiar. And that familiarity brought me comfort.

But I knew I needed to let it go.

I confessed everything I could remember to God, even asking Him to cover the things I had forgotten or didn't want to bring up because I was so ashamed of them. I took my computer out and placed it in the Dumpster by my apartment and refused to have Internet at home for the next several years.

That confession and resulting penance seemed like it was good enough. For the time being anyway.

8

GHOSTS FROM CHURCHES PAST

The confession about the porn and the men and the million other shameful things was the beginning of a spiritual reawakening. Although I wasn't completely convinced that a sovereign, loving God could just sit by and watch a family get abused by His church, and a sixteen-year-old girl get her heart broken by a youth pastor, there was something new inside my heart that caused me to listen and watch for Him.

I figured if He was who He said He was, maybe He'd show me. Maybe *I* would give *Him* another chance.

My best friend, Julie, from Abilene, was going to college at

Hardin-Simmons and decided she needed a mental and financial respite from university life. I had just left my position managing the Christian bookstore to take a better-paying job in communication design at a trendy dot-com. I invited her to live with me in my cute one-bedroom condo outside of Dallas, and a few days later she showed up with her Nissan Sentra packed full of laundry baskets and clothes.

The weekend rolled around, and I got dressed up to go out with some friends. We had plans to go to a few bars and hear some bands, then head to another friend's house to drink and sleep over so we wouldn't have to drive back to our respective homes intoxicated. I asked Julie if she'd like to go along, but she opted to stay behind because partying like that wasn't really her thing.

It was probably seven o'clock in the morning when I made my way back home, where I crawled into my own bed and cursed the amount of drinking I had done the night before. Julie, as consistent as ever, was already awake and in the shower. I had just nodded off when she came out, dressed nicely, and asked me where we were going to church.

How funny of her to assume that we'd still go to church together like we did in high school. Maybe I was ready to give God another try—but church?

Not a chance.

I muttered some expletives under my breath and told her I didn't go to church but there was at least one on every corner, so she shouldn't have a problem finding something to suit her. She left, and when she came back home, I was still in bed.

This pattern continued for a while until Julie finally convinced me to go to church with her. She hadn't yet found a church she was in love with, so I decided if I was going to have to go, I got to choose. We drove up to the Highland Village area of Dallas. A few of my coworkers lived in the area, and I figured if I was going to have to go to church, I may as well make a networking opportunity out of it.

We pulled into the parking lot of a Baptist church. It seemed familiar enough and small enough. I recognized a girl from the marketing department of my company sitting on the far right side of the sanctuary. We took a bulletin from the ushers and made our way to our seats.

I didn't feel as uncomfortable as I thought I would. The music was familiar but fresh. Fully expecting to see someone like my father take the stage for the sermon, I was completely surprised when the pastor stepped out. He couldn't be too much older than we were—maybe in his late twenties or early thirties. And he wasn't wearing a suit and tie.

Julie asked me as we drove home what I thought. Would I go back?

I shrugged.

At best, I was apathetic, still wrestling with the truth of where and who God was. My logical undercurrent told me the best way to be objective as I attempted to discover—or rediscover—my faith meant I needed to stay away from churches. As nice as the people at the Baptist church were, in my mind, they were the ghosts of pastors and church people in my past that I couldn't trust.

It wasn't their fault.

But I still couldn't move on.

We didn't go back to church there, or at least I didn't. Julie may have. However, we did visit a couple of other churches on occasion, usually because of how cute the boys were.

Not too long after Julie had moved in, I found out my department at work was being downsized. On a whim, we decided this change of employment was an opportunity to leave Texas behind. A week after my last day at work, we packed up and moved to Kansas City. After all, we were young—almost twenty-two years old at this point—and, except for my family, had zero commitment to anything in Dallas.

In fact, if anything, I felt haunted as I drove through certain parts of town, being reminded of what happened there and with whom.

Maybe a fresh start is what I needed to find God again.

That is, if He was looking for me.

9

LISTENING

Julie and I both had some friends in the Kansas City area. Two of them, Eric and Chris, were in a band, and they drove down to Dallas in their band's van to help us move. We trekked nine hours back up to the Midwest, where we rented an apartment we had never seen before with a roommate we didn't know very well.

A few weeks after we moved, Eric and Chris's band played at a youth group event at a local megachurch that was Baptist but pretended not to be by calling itself a "family church." It wasn't too far away. And since moving, I had developed a huge crush on Chris. We decided to go.

We walked in, and Julie went up toward the front. I stayed in the back, with an overwhelming sense of panic gripping me. Taking a seat behind a partition, I rested my head in my hands and attempted to get the sense of dread I had from overwhelming me. My heart was racing, and I could feel it pulsating through my body.

More clearly than I have heard God in my life, He said, "*Remember the letter you wrote to Me when you were sixteen? Remember the times you've wondered where I am? I'm here. This is My church, and it's time for you to be a part of it.*"

I told the Voice in my head to shut up. I was probably going crazy. Surely God doesn't speak like that. I thought back to the last time I had taken one of the many pills I would take to feel normal and wondered if it was still in my system.

But then it happened again.

More loudly.

"HEY! Remember the letter you wrote to Me when you were sixteen? Remember the times you've wondered where I am? I'm here. THIS IS MY CHURCH, AND IT'S TIME FOR YOU TO BE A PART OF IT."

Go away! I silently screamed back.

Maybe it was time for another pill. I started fumbling in my purse.

A girl with bright red hair who was about my age came up to me between songs. She introduced herself. "Hi, I'm Kristi. I work here. Can I pray with you?"

For some reason, my panic turned into anger. My skin

began to crawl, and I wanted to run out the doors of the church and never stop. I didn't want to let this random girl in on the dialogue that was unfolding between the voices in my head.

Or the fact that I had voices in my head, for that matter.

What? Why? Who is this girl? No. No, you can't pray with me. I don't think I still believe in your God anyway. Just because I'm in church doesn't mean I have to buy into this crap like you do. Seriously!

But acting nonchalant, like people offered to pray with me every day, I shrugged, casually pushed my hair back from my face, and calmly responded, "Sure. Yeah. I guess so."

She took my hands, but I pulled back. Instead, she put her hand on my shoulder, which tensed up at her touch. She began praying for me, for my friends, and then she said something that made my pounding heart stop dead in its tracks.

"I pray for Anne's involvement with church. With *this* church."

She wasn't trying to manipulate me. Her prayer was very genuine. She was very genuine. I started to get a little more nervous as I wondered why in the world she would pray such a thing for a complete stranger. Later on, I asked her. She simply said she felt like that's what she needed to pray.

Growing up in the South, I learned that even if you don't agree with someone or like them, you could still be nice. So I responded nicely and said thank you. She asked if I'd be up for getting coffee with her sometime. She gave me her phone number, and a few weeks later I called.

Kristi and I became friends, and eventually I started attending the Baptist Family Church (from now on referred to as "the BFC") with her. Chris and I began dating, so he started coming along too.

Kristi worked on the student ministry staff, so Chris and I started volunteering at youth functions. Slowly, I began to fall in love with these teenagers. They made me think of myself when I was in junior high and high school. Their innocence caused me to grieve my own, lost when I was their age. They were seeking a God and a faith they truly believed in. And through them, I remembered what it was like to be found and loved by God and to chase Him on a crazy adventure where anything was truly possible.

I can't recall a specific moment when I finally chose to surrender my heart to God again. That makes me even wonder if there was a specific moment. Maybe it was just a lot of little moments stacked up on top of each other. God didn't prove Himself trustworthy to me in one big burning bush. He didn't guarantee my happiness or take away all my fear in one fell swoop.

But He did find me again.

Or perhaps, maybe I just allowed myself to be found.

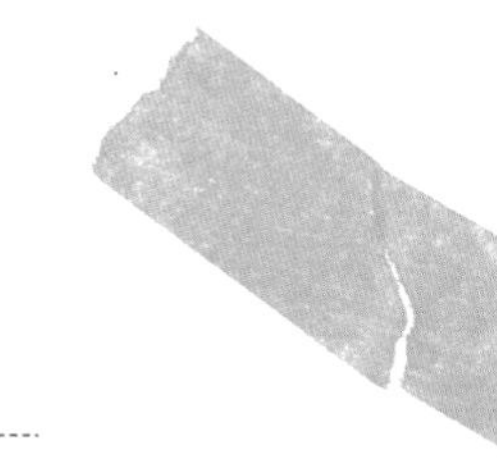

10

FOLLOWING IN THE FOOTSTEPS

My mom was a missionary.

My uncle was a pastor.

My dad was a pastor.

My grandfather was a pastor.

So it would make complete sense that being some kind of minister would take up some space on my résumé. It seems to be in my DNA.

After about a year of volunteering in the student ministry, I was approached about working on staff at the BFC. At first, I said no. Chris and I were now newlyweds, and I wanted to focus on being a good wife. I was also still hesitant about trusting pastors. I wasn't sure if I could take being hurt one more time. Eventually, though, it became clear that serving in vocational ministry was the next step for me.

The youth pastor I worked with was strong in his faith, and trustworthy. He knew when to push us and when to give us time to reflect. I never had met a pastor like him before. His spiritual healthiness was reflected in the rest of our team, and when a group of people is open to the Spirit moving and shaping and growing them, amazing things happen.

And we saw so many unbelievable things happen. We saw students care for their friends who had lost family members to suicide. Families that were broken began to heal. It wasn't perfect, but the movement of the student ministry at the BFC overflowed with grace and compassion for our community.

The church continued to grow rapidly. We went from having four services to ten every weekend. Because of my background in corporate communications, I was asked to take a new position—director of communication and media. The new title (and salary and office) tempted me. I was twenty-four years old and would be the youngest person, and one of the only women, on our leadership team. Ignoring advice from our youth pastor that I wouldn't fit in with the more corporate structure of "Big Church," I followed my own heart's desire and accepted the new role.

As fate would have it, my direct supervisor and I didn't see eye to eye on, well, just about anything. We both had a history in the corporate world, but we were a generation or two apart. Where he preferred independence and micromanaging, I favored collaboration and networking. As a way to branch out and learn from other church leaders, I started blogging regularly. In my musings, I would ask questions about church and leadership. I was just trying to figure it out and find people who were trying to figure it out too.

Evidently, that wasn't a good idea.

I was pulled aside one afternoon and told I couldn't ask questions about theology or church leadership philosophy on my blog, regardless of how generic or unassuming my thoughts were.

You see, if I had said something wrong or asked a question that leaned too far outside of the conservative practices of the church, it would reflect poorly on the church, and ultimately would reflect my faith (or lack thereof) in God, which would in turn reflect poorly on the church for hiring such a faithless, confused person.

Makes sense, right?

I stopped asking those questions. And since I couldn't talk about ministry, my blogging became much more personal in nature.

After our church had a Sunday morning series on sex and relationships, I talked to Chris about an idea I had. Pornography was talked about a little bit in the services, but only from a man's point of view. Maybe I should share my story with addiction. Who knew how many women could relate and heal? Chris agreed it would be a good idea, so off I went to writing.

The first blog went up as a warning of sorts, simply stating that the forthcoming post was going to be a little more "adult" than usual, but there were some topics surrounding sex I thought needed to be discussed. The second post, which told the story of how I became addicted to porn, went up the next day.

The response was beyond anything I ever could have imagined. Not many women talked openly about pornography addiction, and so it became a resource for several people and ministries. I didn't advertise it or e-mail it to anyone I worked with (after all, I still had to look them in the eye at work), but eventually word got around to my supervisor, and once again, I was called to his office.

"Do you really think it's appropriate for you to talk about sex and porn addiction on your blog?"

"Well, after the message on sex last week, and after Chris and I talked about it, I thought it was fine. I had a few people read it before it went up to make sure it wasn't too provocative but was still honest, because there are so many women who deal with this issue silently."

"I don't think it's appropriate. You have teenagers reading your blog. That's how I found out about it. A person in the youth group read it. One of our pastor's kids."

Feeling a bit snarky, I replied, "I was sixteen when I started looking at porn, you know. And I was a pastor's kid. It's just as important for them to hear about it as it is the adults who read my blog. It's just part of my story."

The conversation took a nosedive from there. My supervisor questioned whether I was still addicted—to porn or to drugs ("Maybe I should have you take a drug test," he threatened. "Would we find anything?")—and told me once again that bringing up certain topics in church was not acceptable.

Right.

It had been so long since I had been in the church, I forgot there were certain things that people were expected to keep quiet about.

Like life . . .

I told him I wouldn't blog anymore about sex, and then I started looking for another job—not in a church. I should have gone with my first instinct of staying far away from church and Christians, because I never could wrap my mind around the tension of being who God created me to be in a place that required that I keep the most unique parts of who I was hidden.

Lady Trust

you are so fragile these days, my dear.
like a sickly woman, frail
your skin
paper-thin
bleeds easier than it should[4]

11

THE REALIZATION

Even though I was no longer on the student ministry staff at the BFC, Chris had become the student worship leader, and I'd usually spend Wednesday nights volunteering at our high school service.

At the service one October evening, we sang "Happy Birthday" to one of our youth workers. He was twenty-five. As the final notes of the band played out, I looked around the room and made a heart-stopping observation.

This youth worker was twenty-five. I was twenty-five. My husband was twenty-four. The girl I was sitting next to, a sophomore in high school, was sixteen.

Life had suddenly made a wicked turn, and repressed synapses in my brain began firing. I computed that *I* was sixteen when I was in that "relationship" with the youth pastor, a man who was in his midtwenties.

The realization hit.

My relationship with the youth pastor would be like my husband being in a "relationship" with the high school girl on my left.

I felt sick to my stomach.

I had never given the relationship with the youth pastor much thought after it ended. I talked about it some in premarital counseling before marrying Chris, but I kept it pretty generic. However, this one night shifted my perspective on the significance of the age difference between him and me.

The next day was my day off, and I had *Oprah* on in the background as I was cleaning the house. The guest on the show was a former high school softball coach who had been arrested and convicted of seducing and abusing the young girls on his team. Oprah wanted to get inside his head, and he shared his methods and processes of preying on the girls on his team.

I put down the stack of dishes I was holding in the kitchen and made my way to our oversized couch. I sat down, staring at the screen and listening to his step-by-step recount of how he would first select a child because of her apparent loneliness, especially girls who were new to the team and didn't know anyone. He would make her feel special, earn her trust, and in doing so, she would fall "in love" with him and allow their relationship to continue to a sexual level.

As he revealed each step, I found myself back in 1996, when I met the youth pastor. The way this softball coach lured in these high school girls was exactly how the youth pastor seduced me.

Oprah went on to talk about signs a child might display if he or she is being sexually abused (even if he or she doesn't realize it), and I went to the bathroom and closed the door. While I was splashing cold water on my face, my body began shaking. I looked up into the mirror, and the culmination of the epiphany I had the night before, along with learning how a predator preys on children, caused me to realize that maybe my "relationship" with the youth pastor wasn't a relationship at all.

Maybe I was sexually abu—

I couldn't even think that word.

Abused.

It meant I was a victim. It meant I was violated. It meant I wasn't normal. I now knew something about myself I never knew before, and quite honestly, I felt stupid for not putting the pieces together sooner.

I pulled myself up on the bathroom counter and stared myself in the eyes until time and space no longer existed. Almost ten years of my life became clear, but so unknown to me at the same time. It felt like all of my body's warmth and my soul had been swallowed up by grief. I got lost in the watery pools that stared back at me as the voices in my head only became louder about how stupid I was, how ashamed I should be, and how, if I told anyone about this, people would never respect me again.

Truth was escaping me fast, and fortunately I heard my husband come in the front door before I could go too far into the vacuum of lies that now had opened up inside of me. I pulled myself together and came out of the bathroom door.

"Hey, can we talk about something?" I asked.

"Sure."

"So, you know last night was Grant's birthday. And he's twenty-five."

"Yup."

"And I was sitting next to Claire. And she's sixteen."

"Yup."

"So, remember that youth pastor guy I dated when I was in high school?"

"Uh-huh."

"That would be like you or Grant dating Claire."

"That's just wrong."

"I know. . . . Here's the thing. This sounds ridiculous, but I was watching *Oprah*, and she had this child predator on the show. He went through step-by-step how he would pick his victims and seduce them and make them feel safe and then take advantage of them. Chris, this youth pastor did the exact same thing with me. Every single thing this guy on *Oprah* said happened exactly the same way with the youth pastor. Chris, I think . . ."

My voice trailed off into silence.

Chris didn't say anything back.

"Chris, I think I was abused." The words fought their way out into the air through my rapidly closing throat.

I didn't expect him to say anything back. I mean, what do you say to something like that?

Before he arrived home, I had already decided to talk to a counselor we knew about it.

"I think I'm going to talk to David about it tomorrow."

"I think that's a good idea."

12

LET IT BE

I couldn't sleep that night, and I'm sure my coworkers were surprised when I arrived at the office a couple of hours earlier than I typically would. As a "creative type" at the BFC, I was given liberty to come in at 9:30 or 10 a.m., because we creative types don't like mornings and work late in dimly lit offices.

David worked in a building across the street from the church, so I called him and left him a voice mail.

"Hey, David. This is Anne. I was wondering if you had any time today for us to talk. Something happened to me yesterday, and I need to get some perspective on it. Just call me back if you can. Thanks."

An hour or so later, David called me back.

"Sorry, Anne. I was in an appointment when you called. I do have about thirty minutes free right now before a staff meeting. Can you come over now?"

"Absolutely. I'll be there in just a second."

I drove to the building where he worked and casually strolled into his office like my life hadn't been completely disrupted not once, but twice in the last forty-eight hours. I peeked outside his office door as I went in to make sure nobody had seen me and closed the door behind me.

"You sounded upset on your message," he said. "What happened?"

"I'm not really sure how to say this, and it's going to sound completely ridiculous that this isn't something I'm even sure of, because I just . . . well, I just don't know . . . but . . ." I stammered, avoiding eye contact.

"Whatever you say will stay in this office, Anne."

Taking a deep breath, I hesitantly said, "I think I may have been abused when I was sixteen." My throat started closing again.

"Tell me about it."

"Like I said, David, I realize how stupid it sounds to even say that I *think* I was abused. How do I not know for certain? That's kind of a big deal. And how did I not realize it before? Good gosh. I've worked with teenagers. I've been trained on this stuff. Seriously."

I told him about the youth pastor—how we met, the things he said to me, the things we did, and how it ended.

"Have you talked to him since?"

"Nope."

"Is he still a youth pastor?"

"I don't know, David. I've wondered that nonstop for the last two days, but I've been too afraid to check. I couldn't bear the thought of him doing it to other kids."

"What's his name?"

I told David his name, and he turned to his computer to Google it. After scrolling through a few pages of results, he found him on a faith-based organization's website and pulled up the page.

A photo of him looking the same but older, and now with a wife and kids, loaded with the page.

The shaking came back.

"That's him," I barely whispered, wrapping my arms around myself and curling up into a ball in the chair I was sitting in.

David read the page about what he was doing and where he was. He wasn't a pastor anymore, but he was part of an organization that worked with churches.

"What do you think I should do?" I asked. Scenes from *Law and Order* and courtrooms and having to look his wife in the eyes and his kids watching as he was taken away in handcuffs flashed through my mind and made me sweat. I got dizzy. I didn't know if I could do it.

"Well, I have no doubt that what happened between you was abuse. He was a whole decade older than you. He was an adult. He knew better. Anne, you may have thought you were mature enough to handle it, and you may have consented the whole time, but here's the deal: You were not an adult. You were a lonely teenage girl whose faith was shaken, who had just been pulled away from all of her friends and, at least emotionally, from her family. Especially your father. This guy took advantage of you."

I nodded silently, my body still pulled tightly into a trembling, sweaty ball.

"However, it's been almost ten years. He's serving in a Christian organization and probably has a lot of accountability around him. He's married and has children. I have to wonder if bringing this back up and into his life would cause more harm than good."

I nodded again, a little relieved that maybe I could just accept the fact that this had happened and move on.

"But," David continued, "he obviously caused you great pain. This is going to affect you for the rest of your life, and I would love to help you walk through the process of forgiving him."

"That sounds good," I muttered.

And that's exactly what happened. I told a close friend about it so she could pray for me and the process of forgiving him, and I met with David a few more times. When we felt that I was in a good enough spot, he suggested I write the youth pastor a letter, letting him know I forgave him. I didn't have to send it, as it was mainly for me, but if I felt I needed to send it, I could.

I wrote the letter. Factual. Unemotional. Clearly stating, "This is what happened and it was wrong, but it's been a long time and I need to move on. Whether or not you ever respond, I want you to know I forgive you and am praying for you."

The letter didn't get sent right away. I kept it saved on my computer for about a year. In that year, so many things had happened. The tension between my supervisor and me at the BFC got unbearable, and so I ended up leaving my position there. Chris and I moved from Kansas back to Dallas.

Being back in Dallas brought back some of the haunting memories, and with the memories came bitterness. I prayed about it and felt that I needed to release the letter. I needed to send it to the youth pastor, and with that action felt that I could move on.

I looked him up on the Internet and was taken to the same page and the same photo I had seen in David's office over a year prior. His e-mail address was listed at the bottom of the page. I copied the text of the letter and pasted it into the e-mail, adding the line, "I'm not sure if you ever told your wife about what happened, and I don't know if she will see this e-mail, so if this causes tension in your marriage, please know that wasn't my intent," and hovered over the Send button for a few minutes.

"Are you sure this is a good idea?" I asked Chris.

"I really do. You'll probably never get a response, but I know that's not what you're after."

I clicked the button to send the e-mail, closed down my computer, and walked away.

Maybe now I'd be free of all this shame that had been eating me alive.[5]

13

SPEAKING UP AND INTO FREEDOM

I started wondering if David was wrong about keeping the abuse quiet. Now that it was out, stuffing the past back inside me was like trying to put toothpaste back into the tube. Over and over again I would be reminded of the relationship. Every time I saw a girl who was sixteen, I noticed her innocence and naiveté and wished I could reclaim mine.

I felt the shame cover me like a heavy blanket. It was suffocating me. I wanted to throw it off, to breathe freely again, but keeping David's advice in the front of my mind, I shoved the desire to talk about it back inside.

"Talking about it would only cause more harm than good . . ."

At the time, now twenty-seven years old, I was asked to write an article for a church magazine on forgiveness. A few faces came to mind of people who had hurt me badly in my past: the churches my family was a part of growing up, the supervisor who told me to keep quiet about anything not perfect, and even more recently, forgiving the youth pastor.

I wrestled with the topic for a couple of weeks and finally went back to the magazine's editor with the dilemma.

Without hesitation, she said, "The abuse, Anne. You need to talk about forgiving your abuser."

"Are you sure?" The magazine was mainly read by members of a large conservative church in the area. All my previous experience had told me that you just don't talk about sex in the church. People get offended and upset. It throws them out of being comfortable.

"I'll check with the pastor, but I think as long as we walk through this together in how we share your story appropriately, it could help others heal."

A few days passed, and the editor came by my office.

"He said to write the piece. We'll definitely want to read it as you work on it, since it is such a delicate topic, but he agrees. This is something we need to talk about more in the church."

Are you serious?

A church actually wants to talk about something messy?

Over the next month, the editor, the pastor, and I worked

on the article. We didn't want it to be too full of personal details because the topic wasn't about abuse. It ultimately was about forgiveness. But we still wanted to share the magnitude of the crime that was committed, the sin I had committed by not forgiving him, and what Scripture says about forgiveness.

Inasmuch as a twelve-hundred-word article in a magazine can address a shameful topic and weave it with biblical redemption, this article accomplished it. We all felt that it would be a good piece to help others learn to forgive any kind of offense that was committed against them and, more importantly, understand why we need to forgive.

The magazine released over the weekend, and by Monday, I had a few e-mails in my in-box from people at the church who read it and had been abused in one way or another. The church secretary pulled me aside one day and said she had given the article to a family member who was going through a divorce and having trouble letting go of the pain her soon-to-be ex-husband caused her. By the end of the week, it seemed everyone who read it could relate to it in some way, and people began coming out of the woodwork to seek to forgive others who had hurt them, or, in some cases, ask for forgiveness when they were the people who had caused the pain.

On a quiet Friday afternoon, a girl I had met briefly at church e-mailed me and wanted to know if we could meet. She was about my age. She came over, and I got her some coffee.

"So, your article . . . ," she began, then stopped.

I looked past her demeanor and into her eyes. This girl was hurting somewhere deep.

"Amaris," I responded, "whatever you tell me stays here with me. It's a vault. I promise."

"Well, you see," she continued after a few moments of silence. "I don't know how else to say it. You know what happened to you in the article? It, well, kind of happened to me too. It wasn't a pastor. And I wasn't in high school. It happened when I was in college. I told this guy no, and . . ."

Amaris looked off in the distance with the same look I probably had when I shared my story with David. When you talk about something that's happened to you that you're ashamed of, mentally and emotionally you're swept back into the moment it happened. You get lost in another time.

Attempting to read into the situation, I asked her, "Amaris, were you date-raped?"

She nodded, and her eyes filled with tears. She shared a little bit about what happened to her. And for the first time, with another human being who wasn't a counselor, I shared a little more about what happened to me.

We confessed our darkest secrets to each other in that office. The courage it took to write the article and share my story had resonated in the heart of another who now felt the courage to speak freely.

We cried.

Between the two of us, hidden in our pillows and washed

down our shower drains were probably ten thousand tears from hundreds of sleepless, painful nights.

Tears of shame.

Of remorse.

Of brokenness.

Of pain.

Of desperation.

Of anger.

Of fear.

. . . Of silence.

But that day, what we cried were tears of freedom.

Of grace.

Of hope.

Together, she and I began a journey of wholeness.

Together, we had spoken freely.

I had now seen the redemption and the freedom that occurs when darkness is forced into the light, disguised as awkwardly spoken words. Words that remain hidden in the heart, so terrified to move that when they're released, they carry the power to literally tear down the walls of broken trust and shame.

Filled with a new hope and desire, I realized the church can be safe.

But we can't rely on others to make it a safe place.

It begins with us.

Why are Christians so afraid of honesty? Life SUCKS more often than not. Admit it, deal with it, quit giving pat, "spiritually correct" answers and admit that we don't GET answers to most of our questions, but it's still okay to ask! God watched me suffer through years of sexual abuse - he did not stop it, he did not protect me or rescue me. I don't know why and that makes me angry but people freak out when my anger is expressed in church. So what if I look like the "model" Christian - a BSF Leader, pillar of the church, strong, Godly.... I'm wounded and all the church offers me is pretense, no respite from the evils of this "cruel" world.

Robin

I'm not sure I believe in Hell.
—Korey

I AM HURTING AND
NO ONE IN MY
CHURCH EVEN CARES.

LORY

this feels
fake
& contrived
when we focus
on appearances
- Sam

I WORSHIP
GOD MORE
SINCERELY BY
LOOKING AT
THIS VIEW...
THAN
BEING
A
WORSHIP
LEADER
IN
CHURCH

i spoke up.
the church fired me.

i spoke up.
the church fired me.
-Joshua

God is the only person in the universe that I feel free to be honest with. The only one. I wonder if He visits my church!

Shari

I ♥ it here —
but sometimes I worry
that it's too contrived.
Maybe this isn't what
God had in mind at all.
I wonder, is this REALLY
what He wants from
us?

Felicity

BEEN HAPPILY MARRIED FOR
20 YEARS, BUT IF THIS
OLD FRIEND EVER TRIED TO
KISS ME, I DON'T KNOW
THAT I'D WANT TO STOP HIM.

MOLLY

POST CARD
(printed on recycled paper!)

Even though I am a staff member at my church, most of my DEEP and SIGNIFICANT relationships are with people I've met ONLINE.

-sharon

USA44

To: Anne Jackson
PO BOX 90144
Nashville TN 37209

BLACK PHOENIX TRADING POST
HTTP://WWW.BLACKPHOENIXTRADINGPOST.COM

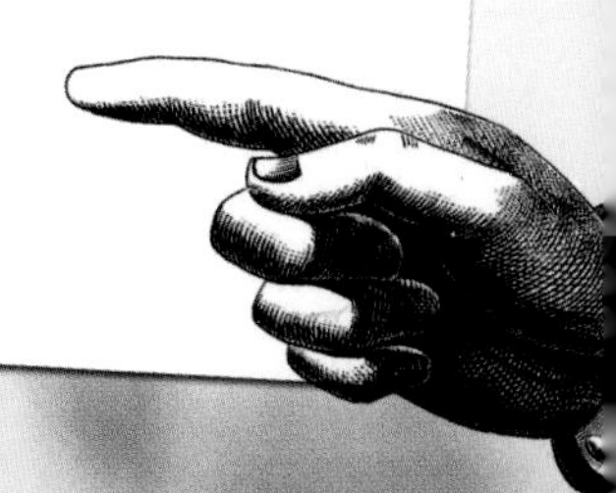

MY BROTHER IS GAY
AND A CHRISTIAN

I DON'T FEEL THAT
I CAN TALK ABOUT IT
IN CHURCH

Andy

I haven't listened to a
sermon in years. Instead, I
write in my journal, read a book,
doodle . . . anything but listen.

Paula

I can't stop I can't stop I can't stop I can't stop I can't stop I can't stop I can't stop I can't stop I can't stop I can't stop I can't stop I can't stop I can't stop I can't stop I can't stop I can't stop I can't stop I can't stop I can't stop I can't stop

Part Two

FINDING SANCTUARY

Naive

Religion is a breeding ground
Where the Devil's work is deeply found,
With teeth as sharp as cathedral spires,
Slowly sinking in.

God knows that I've been naive
But I think it makes him proud of me.
Now it's so hard to separate
My disappointments from his name.

Because shadows stretch behind the truth,
Where stained glass offers broken clues

And fear ties knots and pulls them tight.
It leaves us paralyzed.

But in the end such tired words will rest.
The truth will reroute the narrow things they've said.
The marionette strings will lower and untie
And out of the ashes, love will be realized.

God knows that we've been naive
And a bit nearsighted to say the least.
It's broken glass at children's feet
That gets swept aside unexpectedly[6]

14

BROKEN

If you read the introduction (subtle hint: now would be a good time if you haven't), you know that in May 2008 I posted a question on my blog that simply asked, "What's one thing you feel you can't say in the church?"

I didn't anticipate the response it would receive.

At around five hundred comments, you can imagine the variety of answers. This question obviously struck a chord with a lot of people. I read and reread and reread the comments for months. I printed some out, trying to understand the scope of why so many people felt they couldn't say so many different things in church. Surely there had to be a common denominator.

Fear was obviously there. Shame. Rejection. But those feelings were more of the *why* people didn't speak up more often.

I was looking for the *what*.

What did things like poverty and being gay and worship and money and porn and sex and depression and abuse have in common?

One night in December, seven months later, it hit me:

Brokenness.

Whether it's as a result of sin, or fear of the response we'll get by speaking up about something like politics or relationships or mental health in a broken world, it all boiled down to brokenness.

And if this fracture in whatever part of our lives threatens our reputations, our character, or our dignity, we hide.

If something in our spiritual life is broken or is confusing to us, we hide.

If a relationship is broken, we hide.

If there's an unhealthy habit we fall back on, we hide.

If there's a controversial political or social issue confronting us, we hide.

We ultimately want to hide what's broken, whether it occurs individually or in a community. The Bible is filled with broken people, most of whom at some point or another tried to cover up their brokenness. Yet it seems that the people who are the most broken, the most helpless, are the people God often uses the most.

King David committed adultery and murder, yet he was considered a man after God's heart. Rahab was a prostitute, but she understood her culture and helped protect Joshua's spies. (She later gave birth to Boaz, making her the great-great-grandmother of King David, whose lineage continues on to Jesus.)

The disciples were considered spiritually worthless in their culture and had already been rejected by various rabbis (that's why they were all working in their respective family trades when Jesus found them), and they were the twelve people Jesus most closely associated with.

As you saw from the first section of this book, through church experiences and relationships in my own life as a child and as an adult working in a church, the pressure to be perfect and to have all the answers strongly influenced my decision to keep quiet about a lot of broken things. Some were decisions I was making that were wrong. Others were the result of the sin of others or simply questions about my faith and my God.

Regardless, I know I'm not the only one who has felt the need to stay silent. Chances are you've been exposed to a similar culture of keeping broken things hidden.

We've all seen how dangerous it can be to be vulnerable in the church. But now, we have the chance to do something about it.

15

SANCTUARY

The church is supposed to be a safe place for everybody, especially the people who are the most broken, right? The Bible says the kingdom belongs to the poor in spirit—those so broken they have nothing to offer. Jesus came to heal the sick.

Although unofficial in title, the concept of the church being a refuge dates back to the time of Moses and Joshua. In the Hebrew culture, there are historical records of fugitives seeking protection at altars, which recognizes religion's role in protecting human life even for the most terrible offenders.

The Christian church adopted the right of sanctuary in the

fourth century. Because of Christendom's strong belief in the sanctity of life, clergy and priests began acting on behalf of the criminals, defending them from unfair judgment and execution. It wasn't an easy out for these criminals; they were often restricted in their daily activities, but at least their lives were safe in the church until they received the king's pardon or a fair punishment.[7]

Anyone was welcome to take safety in the church at this time—not only criminals, but slaves who escaped cruel masters and those who couldn't repay debts. Village townsmen, women, and children who came under attack from outlaws could take refuge in the church.

However, as time went by, people with power interfered with the system and began excluding specific groups or crimes. At first, those who had committed treason or murder were no longer allowed to find safety. Over the next few centuries, slowly, fewer and fewer crimes were given the right of sanctuary, until the end of the eighteenth century, when it was abolished altogether.[8]

Outside of the legal system, hundreds of years ago, when a person confessed certain sins or doubted or renounced their faith, some Christians refused to welcome that person back into the church, even if the person had truly repented. These kinds of Christians felt that the church was better with these so-called sinners out of the picture.[9]

I find it interesting that in our current culture, we identify the church as a safe place for broken people to find refuge.

Church is a place for us to claim the right of a modern-day sanctuary where we can name our sins or ask our questions and be protected and sheltered while we search for grace, forgiveness, and answers.

Yet as history shows us, for hundreds of years, churches have been sacrificing the beauty of confession and brokenness for religious trappings and the malady of perfectionism. In some cases, if we don't measure up to a man-made cocktail of moral codes and checklists—if we aren't "good enough"—we no longer feel welcomed in a church or around other Christians.

We feel ashamed.

We feel ashamed that we don't measure up to the "holiness" of others.

And shame tells us to keep those ugly, messy parts hidden.

Without our secrets showing, maybe then we can be accepted.

We think, and in many cases have experienced, that if we share our secrets or our questions, we'll be rejected.

And alone.

And so people—broken people like you and me—feel pressured to choose.

Either we can conform to an institutionalized and over-organized product of religion, masking and repressing our secrets or questions or shortcomings, or we can escape the walls of the church and find a place outside a faith-based environment where we are free to share all of who we truly are.

Over and over again I hear people talk about how they left the church so they wouldn't be judged for their basic humanity.

Most of us choose to live in one of these extremes: conforming or escaping. Few can find peace living in the tension of both. Those of us who do wonder if we're too idealistic to believe a faith community can be a hospital where our wounds are welcomed and can be healed. That true sanctuary can be found both within the walls of the church and outside the church as well.

A Scottish minister once told me, "If you can't be an idealist in a church, then something is extremely wrong."

At the risk of sounding overly idealistic, I'd like to say that for those of us who believe the church should be one of the safest and most grace-giving places a person can experience here on earth, it's time to reclaim what our faith stands for.

It's time for us to politely but passionately disagree with those who make church a "safe" place by removing all the messiness.

It's time for us to put all we have out in the open—not for the sake of faux humility or self-deprecating exploitation or attention, but for recognizing the things the Cross stands for and left for us: ultimate love and undiscriminating grace.

16

A CONVERSATION IN EDEN

It comes as no surprise that many of us keep what we perceive to be the worst and most broken parts of our lives hidden, especially when we begin to mix our free will and sin into the equation. Throughout history, religious leaders were adamant about keeping up the appearance of what they deemed holy. And beyond our outward appearance, there's something that happens within us intrinsically, leading us to hide even from God.

I think back to the story of Adam and Eve told in Genesis 3.[10]

Adam and Eve are in the garden of Eden, living in perfect

harmony with each other and with their Creator. Temptation shows itself, and together they sin, separating themselves from a perfect God.

And they hide.

God then asks them a profound question:

"Where are you?"

I don't think that God was playing a game of hide-and-seek with Adam and Eve. Aside from the fact that He's omniscient and omnipresent, I believe God was asking them a much deeper question:

"Where's your heart?"

And God wasn't asking them because He didn't already know. Instead, He wanted Adam and Eve to uncover the reason they were hiding and be brought to confession. As Matthew

Henry says, "This enquiry after Adam may be looked upon as a gracious pursuit, in kindness to him, and in order to his recovery. If God had not called to him, to reclaim him, his condition would have been as desperate as that of fallen angels."[11]

I'm sure many of us can relate to what happens next. Adam totally ignores an opportunity to confess and instead tries to change the subject, telling God that he is afraid and naked and that's why he was hiding.

God doesn't scold or shame him. Instead, He gives Adam another chance to come clean and confess.

"Who told you that you were naked? Did you eat fruit from the tree from which I commanded you not to eat?"

Adam could have simply said, "Yep. I screwed up. I ate from the tree you told me not to," but instead, he does what so many of us do when we're facing a dead end, and shoves the blame back on God: "*You* gave this woman to me and *she* gave me fruit from the tree, so I ate it" (Genesis 3:12; emphasis added).

If God ever rolled His eyes, this would have been the time.

"Really, Adam? Really? You didn't seem to mind when I gave you this woman to begin with. In fact, you seemed pretty happy about not only the whole woman thing, but the whole naked thing too. And now it's My fault? Really!?!"

Instead, being the kind and gracious God He is (yet still probably rolling His eyes just a little), He turns to Eve and asks her how she could have done such a thing.

Eve follows Adam's modus operandi and points her finger at the serpent that had tempted them.

"The snake tricked me, so I ate the fruit" (v. 13).

This drawing, which was created around AD 1000, perfectly portrays the process of an opportunity to confess.[12] An inquisitive-looking God leans back, wanting to hear Adam and Eve's explanation. The hand under his chin is symbolic of anger. So it's not like He wasn't angry about the situation. But He didn't lash out immediately at their rebellion. We don't see a lightning bolt in his fist, do we?

Adam and Eve pull away from God, looking downward and shamefully guarded; Adam points to Eve, Eve points to the serpent, and the serpent is depicted as unemotional and unaffected by the accusations made against him.

More often than not, we follow this pattern of avoiding God's tender question, "Where are you?" and covering up or shifting the blame. Theologian Scott Hahn sums this up nicely: "The more we need confession, the less we seem to want it."[13]

God's wrath isn't always expressed in anger—that's what we think of when we hear that term. The "wrath of God" is actually better explained as a feeling of grief mixed with a desire to reconnect and restore.[14] And while we think what we've done (or where or who we are) is so terrible, the reason God pursues us in the garden is because He so desperately wants us to be reunited with Him.

He wants to rescue us.

17

A FATHER'S PURSUIT

One of the most recognizable stories in Scripture is of the prodigal son. Countless books and sermons have illustrated the shocking forgiveness given by the prodigal's father after the son returns home, undeserving of anything but instead receiving gratuitous amounts of grace.

This parable has served as an analogy representing the grace we receive from God after we run away from Him, but recently, I've been discovering more and more about the radical implications this story has for us.

Timothy Keller's book *The Prodigal God*[15] has been monumental in helping me extract a deeper meaning of this story and how it so beautifully fits not only the idea of speaking freely, but how it can also encourage us to create safe environments for others to confess by encouraging us to look at where we may be ignorantly hiding self-righteous tendencies.

For those who are unfamiliar with the story of the prodigal son, it's a short parable that Jesus told to the Pharisees—the super-religious people in His day. These people followed the letter of the law but didn't have faith. They were upset that Jesus was spending time and eating meals and being associated with sinners. Cheaters. Liars. The broken.

The "holy" people confronted Jesus and complained, wondering how He—if He truly was who He said He was—could possibly stoop to what they perceived to be the lowest level of humanity and even call them friends.

The Scriptures begin the parable like this:

> Then Jesus said, "A man had two sons. The younger son said to his father, 'Give me my share of the property.' So the father divided the property between his two sons. Then the younger son gathered up all that was his and traveled far away to another country. There he wasted his money in foolish living." (Luke 15:11–13)

All of us can identify with the younger brother in this story. We've all walked away from God. What's interesting to note is the *cost* the younger son's action had for the father. It wasn't like the father had some money in a bank and handed over a bag of gold coins when the son asked for his inheritance. Property was everything to a family. The father actually had to sell off much of what he owned so he could give his younger son what he had demanded.

In this culture, this move was radical. Most fathers probably would have laughed at the request and punished the son for disrespecting his family. But from the beginning, the father showed him unimaginable grace and freedom—he gave the younger son a choice, and after the son made his decision, the father painfully went through the effort to give him what he wanted.

No questions asked. No obligations implied.

He simply handed over what he could so his son could have the freedom to do with it what he pleased.

Many times as we have heard this story, we've allowed the younger son's actions to define what we think the word *prodigal* means. The son ran away from his home, so we assume that *prodigal* means "wayward" or "runaway." A quick trip to a dictionary shows us that *prodigal* actually means "wastefully extravagant" and "recklessly spending money." Which is exactly what the younger son does.

He leaves, goes broke, and ends up feeding pigs for a living. He does it not to earn money, but simply to eat whatever the pigs don't. And he doesn't get anything.

The younger son gets desperate and decides to return home. Because his earlier actions would culturally remove him from his family, he knows he can't return as a son. Rather, he wants to return as a servant.

He plans in advance what he'll say to his father: "Father, I have sinned against God and against you. I am no longer worthy to be called your son, but let me be like one of your servants" (Luke 15:18–19).

The son starts his journey home, and as he nears, his father sees him. Instead of waiting for him to arrive, his father—who is probably a respectable man—runs to greet him. This would be a weird sight for anyone watching. Family elders were usually very reserved in demeanor. Yet the father throws off all worry of appearances and simply can't wait to hold his son again.

The younger son begins his rehearsed confession, "Father, I have sinned against God and against you. I am no longer worthy to be called your son." But before he can even begin to beg his father to be one of his servants, his father interrupts, tells the other servants to get the best clothes, the best jewelry, and the best food ready. There will be a community celebration because his son—not his servant—has returned.

So many times when we sin, we feel like we need to work our way back into a relationship with God. We find ourselves unworthy and shameful. It's difficult to embrace forgiveness. We feel like we have to do something to earn it.

One morning, I was having breakfast with a neighbor of mine. She's a little older than my mom and has experienced more pain and fear than most of us will ever encounter. She and I began talking about the shame and insecurity that I often let follow me around, and she asked if I had considered therapy to help with my self-esteem.

"I've been in therapy on and off for a few years, but not since moving to Nashville," I said. "Not to sound overly confident, but I'm a smart girl. I understand the psychology behind it, and whenever I am in therapy, I know exactly what they're going to say. I know what they'll ask, I know what I'll answer, and I know what their response will be. The problem is I can never get that knowledge to transfer from my head into my heart. It never transforms me. So I decided to save my hundred bucks an hour and just figure it out on my own."

My neighbor reached across the table and put her hand on mine.

"Anne, you can't will yourself to transform. There's nothing you can do to make your heart 'get' it. Nothing. You can prepare for it, and be receptive when it comes, but that's all you can do. You have to step back and let it soak in."

I choked back tears because I realized a few things. One, God wasn't disappointed in me for not making something happen. He wasn't mad because I hadn't figured it out. Honestly, that was one of my biggest fears—that I had somehow disappointed God by not unraveling the mystery of how to transfer the knowledge of His truth from my mind into my spirit.

And two, I was free from that responsibility. Sure, I have to prepare myself by learning the character of God and understanding the depth of His grace. But then I simply need to trust that He will guide me into what my next step is by illuminating something inside me as I continue the process of healing.

You can't will transformation. You and I fail miserably

when we try to work our way out of addiction, shame, anger, or envy instead of letting God work out His way in us.

You've been walking a long way on a journey back home. You're scared to see your Father's face because you know how much pain your sin has caused Him. You're willing to do whatever it takes to be back home, even though you feel unworthy.

Now you can stop.

Let Him run to you. Let Him meet you where you are. You don't have to beg your way back. He never stopped loving you, and after you confess, let Him celebrate your rescue and the beginning of your transformation.

18

THE OLDER BROTHER

Most of us don't think of the older brother in the parable as lost—after all, he stayed with his father the whole time and faithfully obeyed him. But considering the audience Jesus was speaking to, I think the older brother might actually have been more lost than the younger brother.

After the younger brother returns, the older brother hears the party going on and ventures closer to the action to see what is happening. One of the servants fills him in on the details—the return of his younger brother, the celebration, and how happy his father is. But the older brother refuses to join the celebration, and this is a public declaration of disrespecting his father. He throws a temper tantrum. His father leaves the celebration and goes out to meet him, begging his older son to come in. He desperately wants his family to be reunited.

The older son turns down his father and says, "I have served you like a slave for many years and have always obeyed your commands. But you never gave me even a young goat to have at a feast with my friends. But your other son, who wasted all your money on prostitutes, comes home, and you kill the fat calf for him!" (Luke 15:29–30).

It isn't as if the older son is being whiny here. He is extremely upset. His choice of words is vital to understanding what Jesus is communicating to the Pharisees.

"I've served you like a slave . . ."

"I've always obeyed . . ."

The older brother is expressing his feelings of entitlement. The relationship with his father had been one of routine and duty—instead of being a son. Instead of accepting love. He was working his way to his father's blessing but never allowing himself to be loved. Or most importantly, to serve out of that love.

He also distances himself from his brother.

"Your other son . . ."

He could have said "my brother," but he separated his family's unity and bond with his words.

Many of us feel that we can't talk about certain things in the church because of the people in the church who are focused on following rules and earning their way into holiness. In the process, they can become self-righteous elitists who vocally disapprove of the people who have outwardly sinned. Because they're cloaked in moralism, they view themselves as innocent, when in all honesty, they don't even know they are just as far removed from the father as the brother who ran away.

I'm sure you can think of people in your life who have acted like the self-righteous brother. For me, I think of those deacons and their wives who enforced rules without grace. I think of my supervisor at the BFC, who threatened not to allow me back home when he learned about how I had wandered off. I also think about how, because of these people, I've unfairly distrusted others who were genuinely concerned and grace giving, because I was afraid to be rejected again.

There's an important lesson in this for us if we truly believe in creating safe places for people to speak freely.

We can't allow ourselves to be the older brother.

We must do everything in our power, through the grace of God alone, not to be the older brother when someone who has been away comes home.

It's tempting in our fallen nature to say, once we've arrived at a point of moral success, that we welcome people who aren't perfect—but inside our hearts, we judge them ruthlessly.

We look at someone who's screwed up, and we say, "God bless them" or "We'll pray for them," but we don't mourn with them. Pride zealously grasps our hearts, and we celebrate that we aren't the person who messed up. This time, we're safe. We're holy. We're on the right track. Thank God it's not us screwing up this time.

The Pharisees knew the Messiah was coming. They knew people needed a Savior. They just didn't believe that they were the ones needing saving.

This quote from *The Prodigal God* has stuck with me: "Pharisees only repent of their sins, but Christians repent for the very roots of their righteousness, too."[16]

There's a father. There's a family. There's sin that messes up beautiful relationships—with God and with one another.

We should meet the prodigal son as he runs home and run the rest of the way with him. We shouldn't write him off (whether publicly or within the quiet of our hearts) because we think he doesn't belong.

Because you know what? Without grace, the righteous don't belong either.

Sometimes we've been churches that preach a grace up front for those who aren't Christians and grace at the end for those who follow the rules and are "good Christians," but we've tragically neglected the people in between. The truth is that none of us, even on our best, "holiest" days—the days we don't cuss or look at porn or yell at our spouse or at the idiot who cut us off in traffic—even our best days aren't holy enough to be looked at by God.

That's why there's the Cross. And that's why we all need it for both our brokenness and our righteousness.

Found

Emerging from a quiet corner
The one who pursued me all this time
My clumsy hands fumbled in your grace
My eyes aren't used to this light
But now I hear you breathing
And now I sense your peace
I've quieted my selfish mind
And let your love capture me[17]

19

THE VOICES IN OUR HEADS

Adam and Eve embraced their God-given free will and sinned. So did the prodigal son when he left and disrespected his family. Even the older son rejected his family in his pride. They clearly chose to make a decision that didn't align with God's plan. And they chose to hide.

But what happens when the thing we're hiding isn't sin? What if it's something someone did to us, like abuse, or our marriage that's fallen out of shape, or something having to do with our physical or mental health?

When I had the revelation about brokenness being a

theme in hiding, I myself was in the middle of a very broken season in life.

It was something I didn't want to talk about because of the stigma attached to it. And it wasn't because of sin.

It was depression.

Actually, as I write this book, I'm not sure if it's depression or bipolar or a post-traumatic stress disorder from the abuse. We're still trying to diagnose and treat it properly. Either way, it's not something people tend to brag about. There are some funky chemicals in my head that don't like to play nice with each other.

Normally, whatever this "thing" is comes around in October and doesn't leave until February. For some reason, it had taken the previous year off, and because of its prior absence, I had assumed it was gone for good. Why it chooses me some years and not others makes no sense to me.

And that's the thing about mental illness—true, clinical mental illness. It makes no sense when or where or why or how long or even how much.

It just is.

Having been through very dark seasons before, and even having been through very intense therapy sessions before, you'd think I'd know better than to cover it up and let it fester.

Yet that's exactly what I do.

When these seasons hit for me, I become irrational. Not only does most of my faith vanish, but my common sense vanishes as well. It's when I'm weakest. Old habits and compulsions seem to be tempting old friends, offering solace and peace.

Or at least numbness.

And numbness is much more desirable than the hell that was churning in my heart and in the pit of my stomach.

On top of the overwhelming sense of worthlessness and sadness that had been consuming my daily life, a dear family member became sick unexpectedly.

And by family member I mean cat.

(I'm a cat person, okay? I'm sorry. Hang in there.)

Chris and I moved to Nashville when we were twenty-eight. And the molded plastic chair in the waiting room at the veterinarian's office in West Nashville offered little comfort to what was an already uncomfortable day. It was Christmas Eve. My cat had been sick for several days, and it was getting so severe he couldn't eat or drink anything.

This particular cat (we call him "Fat Guy," as he is a rather robust and round fourteen-pound ball of orange fur) is the closest thing I have, and likely will ever have, to a natural child. I fell in love with him on the animal shelter's website, and he fell in love with me when I picked him up out of his cage for the first time. He sleeps on my back most nights and gets territorial when my husband gets too close to me.

If he was sick—as in sick, sick—I don't know what I would do.

But I had an idea of what it might include.

In my bathroom closet sat one white pill in an orange

plastic prescription bottle. It was a painkiller I had left over from a surgery a couple of years earlier.

During my late teens and early twenties, I abused any kind of pill that had any kind of numbing or sedating effect. So knowing my attraction to things that sedate, why did I keep this one white pill so close by?

Because I might need it one day for something that hurt.

You know. A migraine. A bad knee. A pulled muscle.

Or this depression.

This one little pill spoke to me louder than any Bible verse I could read or any lyric to any worship song I had heard.

It promised to take away all the pain.

I was about to give in. If my cat was really sick, I'd go back home, take the pill, not show up to church, and bail on my family's Christmas plans.

All under the guise of a sick cat.

Nobody knowing I was actually the one who was really sick.

I threaded my mobile phone between my fingers as I sat and waited for news on Fat Guy. Fantasizing and remembering what four hours of drugged-up not-feeling would feel like, I began to take note of a little conviction developing in my heart. After all, I had a book coming out in a couple of months about how strong and brave and healthy I was, and here I was, considering falling back on an old addiction to help me cope.

You stupid hypocrite, the voice in my head told me. *You should just take the pill and disappear off the face of the earth. You can't handle this. Remember how easy it was when you were on your own and you could make yourself feel better?*

In a moment of weakness (or should we call it desperate strength?), I text-messaged a friend of mine who's a recovering cocaine addict. If anyone could relate to the feelings of instinctive addiction, I knew he could. And if anyone could talk me out of taking that pill, his voice of experience was probably the only one I'd listen to.

"All I want to do is go home right now and take an oxy," I texted.

No sooner had I pressed Send than the vet came out with some X-rays.

My cat was really sick.

A few moments later, my friend texted back. He simply said, *"I'm sorry. Fight."*

I felt weak. I wasn't sure if I could, but I'd at least try.

20

STUPID CAT

Through tears, I called Chris, who was just about to close down the shop he manages. We'd have to take Fat Guy to the animal emergency hospital for more tests and possibly surgery if we wanted him to recover.

We met at home, where I turned the cat over to my husband and quickly went to help out at the church. I managed to make it through a few services and got to the animal hospital to see what kind of progress had been made.

They needed to keep him overnight and observe him for a few more hours before knowing if he would need surgery. We canceled our flights to Kansas City, where we were planning on spending the holidays with Chris's family, and went home with nothing left to do but wait.

This was certainly not how I had planned my Christmas Eve.

At 5 a.m. on Christmas morning, a call came, telling us that through medication, they were able to fix what was wrong, and Fat Guy, although drugged and shaven in odd places for IVs, wouldn't need surgery after all and would make a complete recovery.

I, of course, was relieved, and we took a late flight Christmas Day to Kansas City. Thinking all the Christmas cheer would wear on me, I continued to believe I'd snap out of this season of depression and nobody would ever have to know.

Unfortunately, that wasn't the case.

Another couple of weeks passed, and the darkness only became more and more powerful. At some point, I caved in and took the pill.

Sure, it gave me a little bit of the buzz I was hoping for, but even it wasn't strong enough to cover up the shame I felt for taking it.

What was happening wasn't fair to my husband. It wasn't fair to my coworkers or my friends. After church one morning, Chris and I went out to eat, and I told him he needed to leave me. He'd be better off without me. He could make me out to be the bad guy, and I wouldn't put up a fight.

I just wanted to be alone.

And I wanted more drugs.

The thing about my husband is, well, he's a lot smarter than me. And at this point, we had been together for eight years.

Eight years is way past the limit where you sugarcoat the truth.

Over some mildly appetizing Italian food, he said, "I am not leaving you. This is your passive-aggressive way of telling me that *you* want out. You're being completely selfish."

I argued how he could find a much stabler, happier person than I could ever be. That when I was alone, I was a better person too. Nobody should have to carry the weight of my depression but me.

He didn't buy it.

Instead of telling me everything was going to be okay, he sternly told me he loved me and that the following Monday morning I was going to call my doctor and we were going to discuss my getting back on medication.

I resisted.

It didn't matter.

So I got angry.

21

THE VALLEY

Even though the one thing I desired was to be by myself, deep down, none of us wants to be alone. The reason we crave isolation so badly is because more than our fear of being alone is our fear of rejection.

Funny how that works.

The reason I didn't want to confess my struggle was that I didn't want to be rejected by anyone, including my husband. So even though I shared a little bit of what I was going through with him, essentially I rejected myself for him by telling him to move on. I couldn't bear the pain of what I imagined his "real" rejection to feel like.

As easy as it is to always point the finger at the church or at the friend who betrayed you as the source of you keeping your secrets hidden, claiming that their judgment would be too much to bear, and as valid as those reasons could be, we are still the ones who make the conscious choice to stay silent.

It's a decision we make.

And I think many times we keep our secrets hidden not only because we fear rejection or being alone, but also because we fear change.

I knew the work that was ahead of me—the prospect of medication and side effects, of counseling, of going back to deal with the issues that can trigger my depression—was hard. I didn't want to do it.

I didn't want to change. Popping little white pills that numb me for four hours at a time would have been so much easier.

We don't want to change, so we think it's easier to pretend that nothing is going on, when in reality, a war of crisis is raging inside of us.

We put our masks on because we assume everyone else is, and we use the *F* word.

Fine.

Everything in life is fine.

But it's not.

And guess what?

It's okay that everything in life is not fine.

In fact, it's okay that quite possibly in your life right now, nothing is fine at all.

Your fears may be valid, but you can't let them dictate the course of your actions.

It took all the willpower I had to walk into that doctor's office and talk about medication options.

Literally.

I had no more strength.

I needed to borrow some from others.

My husband let me use some of his. Another friend came alongside me. As I began to write about my journey online and shared about it when I'd speak at churches, more people surrounded me in prayer and support.

And then something beautiful began to happen.

I started to hear "Me too."

Other people were out there in the same Valley of Death I was walking in, but we were all surrounded by so much darkness we couldn't see one another. And the darkness told us we couldn't speak up.

We were all just waiting to know we weren't alone. We were waiting to be rescued. And it took someone first saying, "I'm broken," for the others to hear that voice and realize we were surrounded by others just as broken as we were.

Just because somebody speaks out doesn't instantly fix anyone, and that's the way it is sometimes. We can't always expect life to be perfect once we've confessed or discovered we aren't alone.

But sometimes that's just enough to get us through another day.

22

HOPE FOR A BROKEN HEART

The word *confession* conjures up ideas of dark wooden booths in old churches, or even secret wrongdoings we need to get off our chests.

To some extent, those pictures are accurate, but they don't fully define what confession is.

Confession by its simplest definition simply means speaking truth or agreeing with what is true.

Sometimes the truth takes ugly shapes, like when we sin or when we're violated or betrayed by another person. But other times, truth is something beautiful, and it's important for both kinds of truth to be spoken.

Speaking this lovely kind of truth is essential in our quest for finding freedom. I think of the psalmist and how many times he found himself terribly hopeless and lost, wishing for his death (or wishing other people would die). Over and over again, he'd end up back where he started, finding evidence of God's faithfulness and provision, and then declaring it out loud.

We've already seen how a person's confession can lead others to find courage to speak freely about the darkest parts of their hearts. It works the same way for good things too.

How many times have you been encouraged by reading a story in the Scriptures or hearing a story of how God has been faithful in someone's life? Doesn't that kind of confession move your heart along to search for the same kind of hope?

Not long ago, I discovered I had an arrhythmia in my heart that caused it to beat twice, sometimes three times, as fast as it normally should. My husband and I were visiting some friends in Scotland who were starting a community outreach, and we wanted to climb to the top of the highest hill in the city to pray over the city with them. A few hundred yards in, I couldn't breathe, and my chest started hurting.

While I sat down on a nearby rock to rest, James, our friend, and my husband continued climbing (I assured them I was fine). Another friend, Geoffrey, stayed back with me, as I apologized profusely for being so incapable of such an easy climb. As a man well into his seventies jogged effortlessly by us, I decided I needed to make some serious changes in my sedentary life.

A couple of years passed, and I lost some weight, but exercise never got any easier. My heart would race as soon as I'd exert myself, and if I pushed for more than just a few minutes, I'd almost pass out. It took me an hour to recover every time.

After seeing a handful of cardiologists, I still didn't have a solid diagnosis. All I knew is that it wouldn't kill me. Which, I suppose, is good, but being twenty-eight years old and not able to walk six blocks without passing out wasn't exactly my idea of the active lifestyle I wanted to lead. I wasn't satisfied, so I took matters into my own hands.

I sweet-talked an appointment setter at the doctor's office into letting me see one of Tennessee's top electrocardiologists. When he entered the room, I thought he looked like a more mature, more doctorly version of Kenneth the Page from the TV show *30Rock*, golden blond hair hanging diagonally right over his eye.[18]

He reviewed all the tests I had been given over time and looked up at me and said, "It's textbook. You have a condition called supraventricular tachycardia, or SVT for short. We can fix it by going into your heart and burning the extra electrical pathways you have. That solves the problem in over 90 percent of people."

Someasaywhatacardiawhatdidyousay?

"So that's it?" I responded. "How do you know?"

Kenneth the Page Doctor explained how the electrical system of the heart works and the symptoms I had, and I believed him. It seemed like a minor procedure: they would insert some catheters in my leg, feed some wires into my heart, trigger the arrhythmias, and ablate (or burn) what shouldn't be there. He acted like running wires through someone's leg and into their heart and then burning pinhead-sized lumps of cells was as easy as taking out the trash or assembling a nightstand from IKEA.

"The risks are really low, especially for someone in good health like you. The worst-case scenario, other than death, [*Gee, thanks*], would be we would burn a spot too far and actually burn one of the conductors that's supposed to be there. If that happened, we'd have to insert a pacemaker."

That's not really that big of a deal, I thought, reflecting on my friend who's in his early forties and has a pacemaker and runs marathons twice a year. "It's better than what I have now," I said.

"Well, go home and think on it. Do some research. And if you decide to have it, just call me and we'll get it scheduled. There's no rush—it won't kill you."

I went home and Googled the procedure and read about people who had it done who went on to live healthy, active lives. Of course, on the Internet you always find one or two hypochondriacs claiming it was the worst thing they've ever experienced, but overall, it seemed like the results from the surgeries were really positive. The National Institute of Health reported a 90 percent permanent cure rate for most patients, and with the specific kind of SVT I had, the percentage was closer to 98 percent.

I scheduled the appointment and wrote a blog about what would be happening, asking people for prayers. The surgery seemed fairly low risk considering I'd have wires in my heart, but I was still nervous.

People responded kindly, and there were quite a few who had the surgery done or who had a friend or family member who had the same kind of procedure. Their e-mails flooded my in-box, telling me what to expect.

I realize every circumstance is different, and God and prayer aren't magic pills, but the combination of people's prayers and support as well as their own stories of surviving the surgery and living dramatically better lives encouraged me.

These people confessed truth in many ways—their prayers that God is ultimately sovereign and in control of the surgery, and how He had been faithful in many similar ways before. I may have been rolled into that operating room alone, but inside my head were scores of people's voices supporting me as I was sedated and my heart was zapped with tiny little wires.

I woke up a few hours later in a recovery room, exhausted from the sedation but feeling well. After I stabilized, the nurses took me to a hospital room where I'd be staying overnight. Kenneth the Page Doctor came in and told me how the surgery went.

"First of all, when you said your heart rate was hitting 180 beats per minute, well, that was an understatement. When we triggered your arrhythmias, it shot straight up to 220 to 240 beats per minute. We not only found one extra conductor—we found two. One we were able to burn off entirely, but the other was too close to your AV node, the one you need, so we froze it off as well as we could. I think you should be fine."

And fine I was. A little over a month later, I checked in with him and told him how I had been feeling and how my heart rate had been acting. It still wasn't perfect, but it would take time to reshape my heart muscle into acting the way it should.

So many people confessed truth over me during this season. They spoke words of love and healing, of encouragement and hope. Words of faithfulness and peace. They promised to pray for me, and they brought me meals and sent cards and flowers. Some showed up at the hospital or called. They confessed the truth of friendship and community, and that was a gift I needed to open—not only for my physical heart, but for the heart that was still having problems accepting friendship and love. The heart that still had some walls built up.

Now that I'm through that trial, it's my turn to share that hope—the hope that was given to me through the encouragement of others. Because once someone gets a gift like hope, that person has a responsibility to pass it on.

To give it away.

I can promise you this: if you don't need hope right now, there's someone around you who does.

And if you are the one who needs hope today, please take whatever you can of mine.

There is a light at the end of the tunnel. There is a God who is faithful to give you exactly what you need. Whatever it is.

He'll provide what you need, when you can't handle things anymore. Whatever happens may not look like what you expect or come at a time when you think you need it most, but in the end, I promise you—I confess to you—He's faithful.

I believe that so much, I'll bet my heart on it.

23

WHOLE AND HEALED

I heard somewhere once that during Billy Graham's crusades, after he finished his message, he returned to a chair and closed his eyes and prayed. From what I understand, he didn't want to see how many people were (or were not) coming forward; he just wanted to pray for what was happening.

Granted, I never went to a Billy Graham crusade, and I am probably a terrible Christian for even admitting I don't know that much about them to validate if this actually happened or not.

However, as I've had the opportunity to speak at several churches in a variety of services, I've noticed how easy it is to get caught up in how people are responding and thinking it has something to do with me.

Recently, I spoke at a college and young adult service about the freedom that comes with confession, the healing that takes place when we share our brokenness with others. At the end of my talk, I turned the service over to the pastors and leaders at this church to pray with anyone who needed it.

I walked off the stage, sat in a chair, and buried my head in my hands, praying for the people at the service while trying to overcome the temptation to look around.

I assumed that since I was a guest speaker, the people at the service would feel more comfortable praying with the pastors they knew, but a few moments after sitting down, I felt a hand on my shoulder. I sat up, expecting to see a staff member or maybe someone to take my microphone, but instead was met by the tearstained face of a beautiful young woman.

I leaned over to hold her for a moment, and her body began heaving in my arms as she wept. Her tears rolled off her face and landed on my jeans, one by one. I could feel them as they drenched the denim and melted onto my skin.

Pulling back from her, I asked her what her name was and if there was something I could pray for her. Given the story I shared from the stage, about the addiction I faced when I was in my teens and twenties, I assumed she needed to confess something about that.

But what came out of her mouth surprised me.

"I just don't feel like I'll ever be good enough."

I've felt healthy enough for a few years to talk about addiction, but the feeling of insecurity and worthlessness is a chain of mine that I wonder will ever break.

Inhaling deeply, I leaned back in, silently begging for words of truth. Scriptures I don't even know by memory began to flow out of my mouth and my heart. I felt as if I were praying them not just for her—but for me.

When I confessed the lies she said were in her head (not good enough, not worthy enough, will never be enough), I discovered I was confessing them for me as well. The same happened when I confessed the things that are true about us and God's grace and love for us. This confession was for both of us.

There's a passage in James that talks about healing in the expression of community: "And the prayer that is said with faith will make the sick person well; the Lord will heal that person. And if the person has sinned, the sins will be forgiven. Confess your sins to each other and pray for each other so God can heal you. When a believing person prays, great things happen" (5:15–17).

Sounds simple, right? James was writing this letter to the early church, a group of people who lived in constant relationship with one another. They literally shared everything they had—meals, homes, money, time. If someone was sick or had been screwing up or if something was wrong, simply because they spent so much time together, it would have been obvious to the rest of the community that things weren't in harmony.

This scripture not only addresses physical sickness, but

the sickness that comes when we've separated ourselves from God. The first time James uses the word *heal*, its original meaning in the Greek is a physical health or wholeness (v. 15). The second time, after he talks about confession, the kind of healing that he refers to is the healing that happens when a burden is lifted or carried away from someone (v. 16).

Interesting.

I was supposed to be there to help other people confess . . . to help other people take a step into freedom.

Yet this confession was a beginning—not an end for this lovely girl *or* for me. Someone once told me that there is a difference between admission and confession, and I think that's important to recognize. Admission is just sharing something that's wrong so you can get it off your chest. Confession, on the other hand, is the beginning of transformation.

When you confess something that's shattered in your life, something that you've kept hidden, you're acknowledging that you need the Cross. You need God's grace, and you're willing to allow it to find you as you seek the truth.

It just goes to show how powerful confession is, because here I was with a complete stranger, and we were both confessing, praying, and beginning a path of healing together. We were confessing the broken—that we weren't enough and we were afraid. That we didn't trust and we were ashamed. But we were also confessing the truth that God was bringing healing to us, and as the passage in James says, we were living life—in that present moment—whole and healed.

I CONFESS
THAT I AM A HETERO-SEXUAL MALE
THAT I PURSUE GIRLS WHOM I AM SEXUALLY ATTRACTED TO
THAT I FIND THE ABSTINENCE CULTURE HURTFUL AND USELESS
THAT I HAVE NO GUILT IN THESE MATTERS
GOD SO HELP ME. AMEN.
JOEL

Anne-

God - all ears that can hear.

My confession is of my girl. Her name would be Bella. She is now in heaven with her Father, our Lord. I was told I couldn't and most certainly shouldn't have her. At 20 years old with an abusing boyfriend, two parents with brain tumors and a debacle called my life I made a decision on Oct. 30 of 2002 that has been seldomly revisited.

I had an abortion.

"Bella" or "Isabella" means consecrated to God. I found that out long after I named her and I know now that she was indeed set apart by Him.

My life has been forever changed.

I pray it brings Him glory, some day, some way!

♡-Natalie

I confess,
I had an affair on
my wife, and I still
think about the other women.
Steven

I'm addicted to Porn.
&
It's crushing my soul.
Matt

I am not afraid to die.
I am afraid to live.
I am afraid to fail in my
God-ordained responsibilities.

God, are You there to heal
The damage?

— Joe

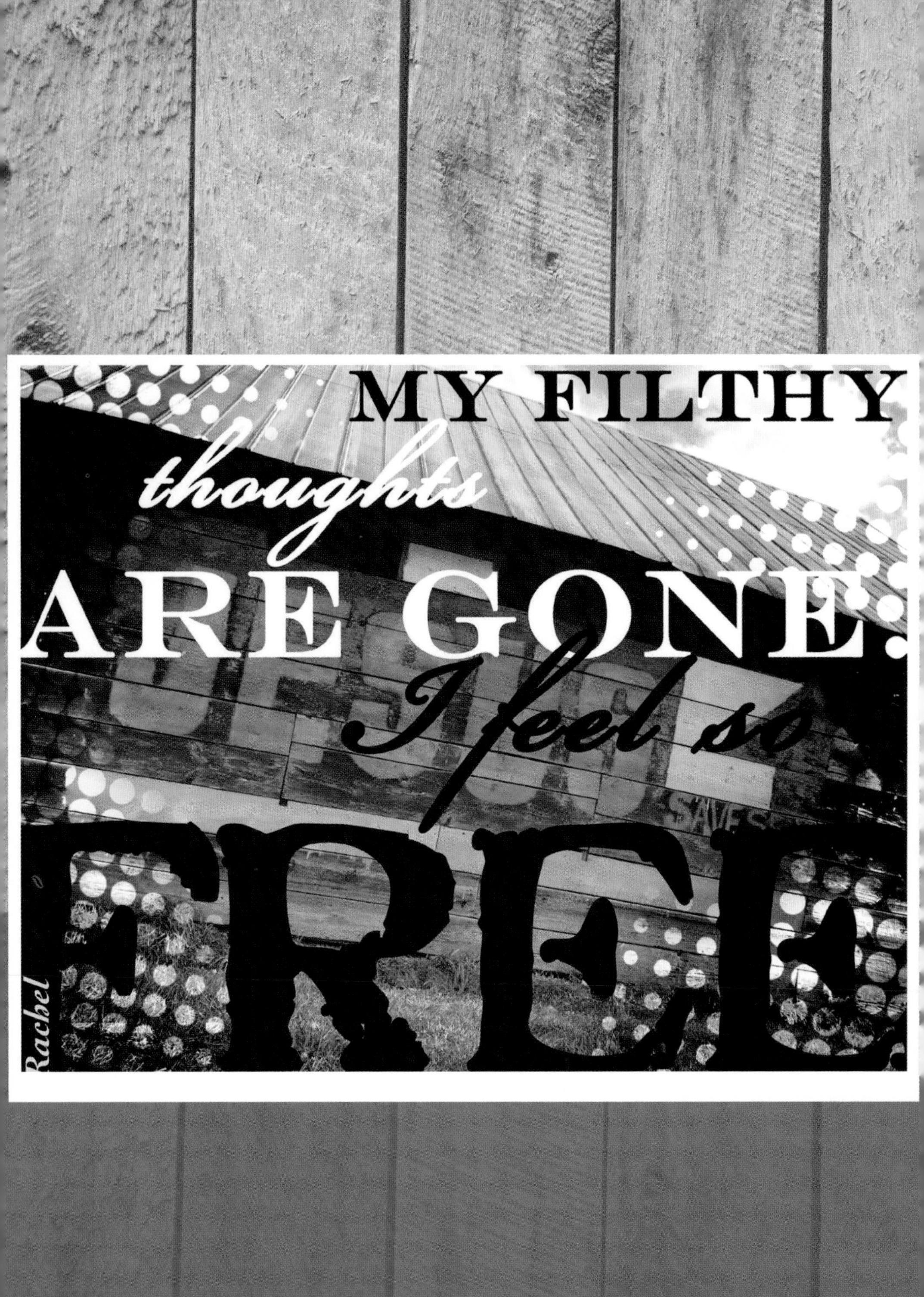
MY FILTHY
thoughts
ARE GONE.
I feel so
FREE.
SAVES
Rachel

I wish our church
was multi-ethnic.
-Tina

I AM AFRAID THAT GOD'S PLAN FOR
MY LIFE INCLUDES BEING SINGLE
AND THAT I AM NOT STRONG
ENOUGH TO BE HAPPY AND
CONTENT WITH THAT.
AMISA

I'M A
DEMOCRAT.

Date:

Rx Every time I treat a child who has a terminal illness, I become more certain that there is NO "Master Plan"

Qty: ______
Numeric

Qty: ______
Alpha required for CS Rx's

Signature (Required)

PRINT NAME Danielle	Refill X
DEPT.	NPI#
~~DEA BU 529 4448~~	

PHARMACY LABEL

Test Area:

How do you tell a "No"
from simply no answer?
Is God even getting
my prayers?
FIRST CLASS

Notes

I've lied so many times about
who I am,
what I like,
the things I know and understand,
where I've been,
what I value,
how well I've done,
and what I believe
that I don't really know myself.
And the parts I do know—
in light of all that I wish I were instead—
I really hate.

—Molly

Brittany

I was raped, by a coworker...
I thought he was a friend

Amy

I struggle with a lack of desire
to have sex with my husband.

Honestly, I don't feel confident at the moment and I need support. Help me and don't think less of me.

Jay

My marriage wasn't working, but I was the pastor. Who could I turn to?

– Jonathan

I can't say I have thought about divorcing my husband or being with another man other than my husband

Mary

- I give sex to get love.

Ashley

I don't trust that God truly has my best interest at heart.

I am fearful to completely abandon myself to Jesus and allow Him to control my life. I've been following Him for 10 years.

– Dan

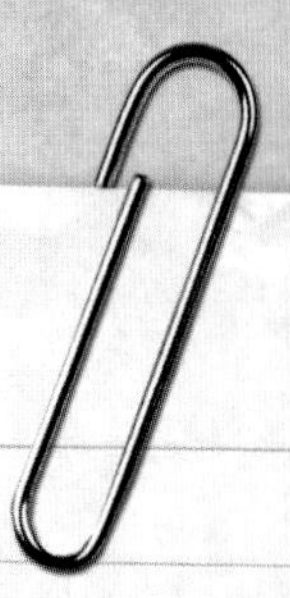

The Bible wasn't written for people who don't actually believe God's Word is Truth. So making the assumption that everyone else believes in the Bible or in God is really insensitive and arrogant.

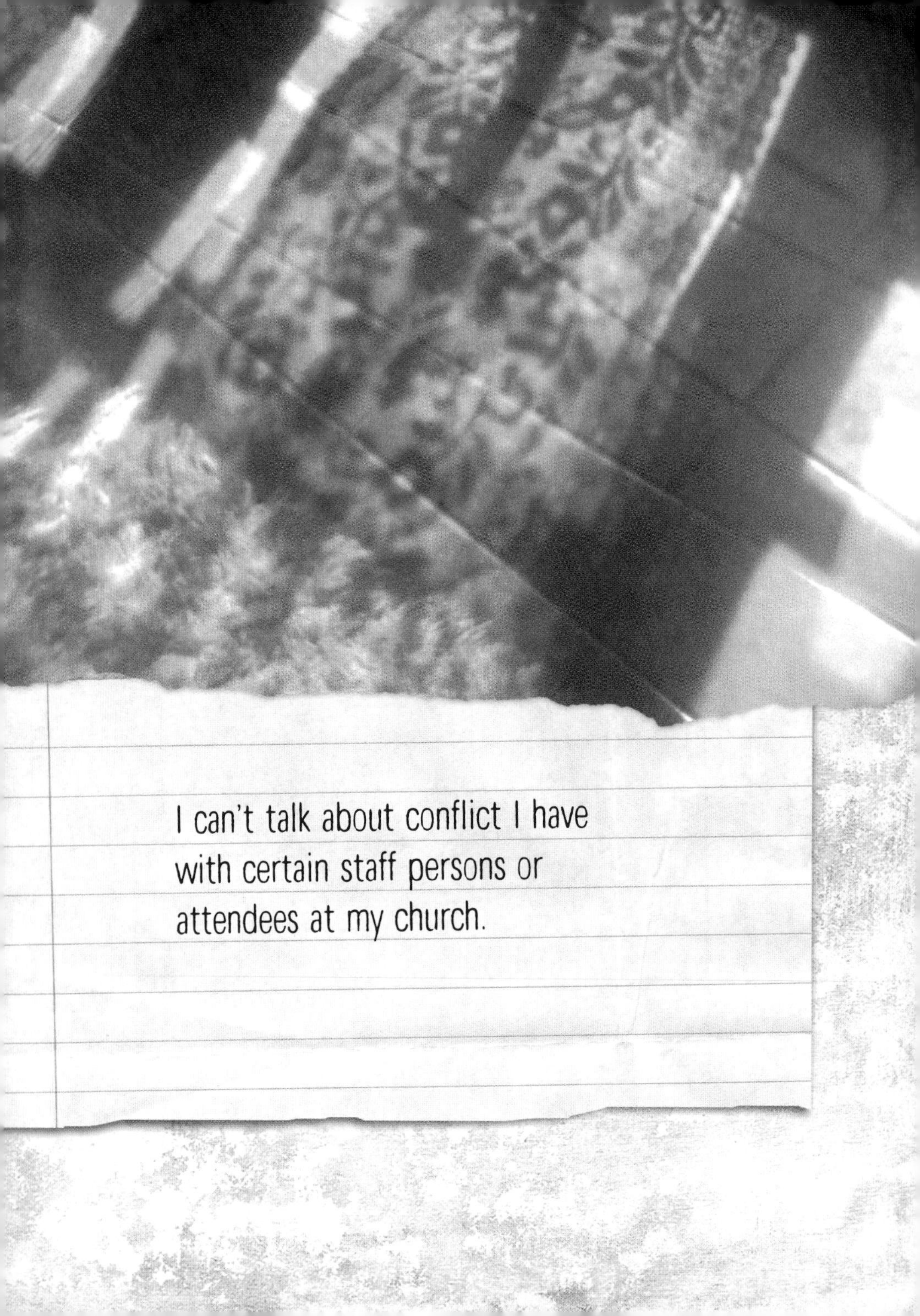
I can't talk about conflict I have
with certain staff persons or
attendees at my church.

I can't say I have questions about the existence of **God**.

I have never experienced Christian community within the Christian community. The closest I have ever gotten to experiencing Christians like community is within Alcoholics Anonymous.

—Jane

Part Three

A PRECARIOUS PATH TO FREEDOM

The Rescue

When I was younger,
nineteen or so
and needed to be rescued
I stopped by the liquor store on Green Oaks
and bought a small bottle of vodka.

they never carded me.

I'd continue down the curvy road
down to the place where people parked their boats
and I'd hide my car, and walk down to the dock.

Like a buoy, the dock would raise up, raise down
with each roll of the lake from the night to the shore
and I'd walk to the end, where I'd lay flat on my back
in the silence and with the stars
letting the vodka warm me
as I continued to bob up and down
with the lake and the dock.

I suppose I hoped that my rescuer would find me
and hear the quiet screaming of my heart:
alone! afraid! lost!
and he would simply sit next to me
his hand on my knee or my arm or my face
and with his presence I'd know that
in the end, when I'd sober up and leave
that everything would at least be a little bit okay.

For a couple years I did this
even when I moved two hours away
I found my way to the dock several times
waiting to be rescued
and looking to the stars for hope.

A decade past, there are still moments
when I want to lay on my back on the dock
a thousand miles away

although now, I know my rescuer is
and was and has always been

Yet the stars still bring me hope
and with them I'm reminded
I am not alone, even in times
when the loneliness is loud

Because we all seek out the star
that guides us to our rescue;
captivating us with a holy
gravitational force. [19]

24

THE GIFT OF GOING SECOND

It was fall, so the sun began to set before four o'clock in the afternoon. The temperature dropped dramatically when the light disappeared. On my way out the door, I grabbed a jacket and a scarf. My West Texas upbringing left me ill equipped for temperatures below seventy degrees.

I was on my way to a concert that was a fund-raiser put on by high school kids every year. My husband's band was playing, and I was looking forward to spending some time with some students I was volunteering with.

Crystal was one of those students. She was shy and

admittedly insecure at times, but I could tell she was beginning to find herself, and on rare moments, she also was finding the confidence to let herself shine through.

We grabbed some soda and sat down at a table off in the back of the room. She was quieter than usual. I asked if everything was okay, and she assured me she was fine. It had just been a long day. The first band started, and the bad PA system echoed their music throughout the sports complex in their gym.

Between songs, I kept glancing over at Crystal. She wasn't paying a bit of attention to the band, the music, or the swarms of people milling around us. She was intently focused on staring at the top of her Diet Coke can. A few other girls joined us at the table for a while, and she barely looked up.

Something was definitely wrong.

I may not be good at much, but something I feel I've been uniquely gifted with is a very keen sense of reading people. Call it intuition or a sixth sense; I don't know. But when something is wrong with a person, as I was sensing with Crystal, it's almost like I can hear the sounds her heart is too afraid to turn into words.

Crystal was a good girl. She never got in any trouble at church or school. I couldn't imagine she was feeling guilty for partying too hard or getting into a fight with someone.

And then it hit me, right out of the blue.

She had a porn problem.

I know it sounds weird, and trust me, I don't typically

walk into rooms and think, *Oh, she has a porn problem*, or *Oh, he's cheating on his wife*, but sometimes those things just hit me; and most of the time, my instincts have been spot-on.

The question now was how to find out for sure. Because if my gut was right, this meant our relationship would grow much deeper, very quickly. And if I was wrong, well, I'd look like a freaking idiot.

I had already asked her if something was wrong, and she said no, so I didn't want to seem like I was pushing her. My next thought was to simply share how porn had been such a problem in my own life, but then I realized how creepy that would be—especially if I was wrong. How do you start that conversation exactly? Especially at a high school rock show? I played the conversation out in my head.

"So, that song was really awesome. That bass player is incredible. Did you know I was addicted to porn? Wanna hear about it?"

Yeah.

That probably would be just a tad awkward.

Silently, I asked for wisdom and courage to say the right thing. Actually, it didn't even have to be the right thing; it could have been anything to help my friend get whatever she needed to get off her chest.

The first band finished, and I asked Crystal if she wanted another Diet Coke. I got up and got more snacks and came back. She was still looking pretty upset. I decided to just dive in and let the conversation flow.

"So I've had this thing that's been really jacking with me

lately. It actually used to mess with me a lot a few years ago, but it still tempts me on a frequent basis. . . . I really haven't been able to share much about it with many people, but I feel like I need to share it with someone."

I paused a bit, taking a mental and emotional deep breath, realizing that I was just about to confess something really shameful to a girl I barely knew. At this time, the secret about my porn addiction was still very much close to my vest.

"You can totally say no. I mean, I know you don't really know me and stuff, but I just feel like I need to share it with you."

Crystal looked confused, and rightly so. She had one of her eyebrows cocked up and her mouth twisted a bit, but I could tell she was curious.

"Sure, yeah, I guess . . . ," she mumbled, looking down.

"And you won't tell anyone about it, right? Because I'm not really sure how many people I want to know about this."

She now looked a little concerned, like maybe she needed to pull out her cell phone and have the police on speed dial.

"No, I won't tell anyone," she said, now trying to mask her *What the heck?* look with a *You can trust me and I'm serious* expression.

"Okay. You see that guy up there tearing down the drums on the stage?"

She looked up and nodded.

"His shirt says XXXChurch.com—The #1 Christian Porn Site, right?"

Crystal wrinkled her nose a little bit. "Yeah, what is that, even?"

"It's a website for Christians who have addictions to porn and sex and stuff like that."

"Really?" she asked, whispering. "A lot of Christians look at porn?"

I leaned in a bit and nodded.

"That's kind of the thing I wanted to talk to you about. That website has actually been really helpful for me, because when I was in high school and up until a couple of years ago, I was totally hooked on porn. Well, I was hooked on a lot of things. But porn was the biggest issue for me."

Crystal looked back at me, not blinking. Not saying anything. So I continued talking.

"You see, I got rid of my computer a few years ago, and even right now I don't have Internet at home, but I have it at work and when I go over to my in-laws and stuff. So now that I have access to it, I'm finding that I keep getting tempted to look at it again. The cool thing about XXXChurch.com is they have software called X3Watch you put on your computer and it will e-mail the sites you visit to people you tell it to, you know, for accountability. And since I'm starting to be tempted again, I really need someone to help me keep that in check. I know it's a big ask, but can I put you down as someone who would be e-mailed my Internet usage report?"

I didn't mean to confess *that* much. I totally didn't plan on telling her all that. I didn't plan on asking for her help.

She simply said, “Sure. I guess that’d be fine,” and turned her head back toward the stage. My husband’s band was about to play.

It wasn’t the reaction I was expecting. I was sure she was going to confess something back to me. But maybe my gut instinct was wrong. Maybe I needed the help and it wasn’t about her.

Chris’s band played a few songs, and Crystal and I sat at the table in silence. I felt terrible for making her feel so awkward. After they were done with their set, I made the decision to apologize to her.

Steve, the lead singer of my husband’s band, started singing the last song, an acoustic and musically moving piece called “Silence.” Tears started cutting a path on Crystal’s porcelain skin as he sang.

Late night trying to find escape
The memories and thoughts that chase you
Out into the light
Of the place you try to hide
Face to face with all the proof
You swear they’re looking down on you
They look so deep inside
And you tried so hard to hide
And now you break your promise to yourself
You storming through the dark
And needing someone else

The mystery
The tragedy
And of pulling up those you find
Inside the only hand
That's in sight
I need someone to fight for
I need someone to speak
I'm lost and abandoned
And the silence is killing me
I need to feel human
I need to feel anything
I'm lost and abandoned
And the silence is killing is me [20]

Steve thanked everyone, and the band started to head offstage. Crystal swung around the table to face me with such force our cans of Diet Coke rocked back and forth, threatening to spill.

She leaned in so close I could feel her breath on my neck as she said, "What you talked about earlier? The porn? That's me. That's me too. I can't stop. I look at it all the time. On the Internet. On TV. However. I can't stop. I saw my brother's *Playboy* when I was ten years old—that was eight years ago—and I haven't been able to stop since then. I thought I was the only girl who had this problem. I knew guys looked at it. In fact, it kind of seems expected when guys look at it. I thought I was so messed up. I know it's not right, but I've never been able to tell anyone about it. Anne, I need to stop. I have to stop." Her body shook as she cried, and I wrapped my arms around her neck and pulled her close to me.

"You think we can help each other with this?" I asked her. "Would you want to put that software on your computer too, and then we can just talk about this? Maybe find some other things to help us?"

She nodded her head yes, and her body seemed to almost float off the table. Sure, this confession was just the beginning of a very long, very difficult road of finding freedom, but the weight that had been bearing down on her for the last eight years of her life had lifted. The air she now breathed in and that passed through her blood and through her heart was no longer polluted by the shame she had been carrying.

What transpired at this concert is what my friend Jon calls "the Gift of Going Second."[21] Whenever somebody confesses something, and they're the first to do it, it's usually a pretty hard step to take. They don't know how people will respond. They fear all the judgment and isolation. But they do it anyway. They give a gift.

What happens on the other side of that confession is something beautiful. When you confess, there's somebody on the other side of that confession who could very well be keeping a secret too. So when you go first, you're opening up this amazing opportunity for trust. You're saying, "I'm broken." That trust carries so much power with it. It can give people the courage to go second.

When people go second, it's not an easy thing, but because

you've already broken the silence—you've already released some of the shame in that confession—it makes it a little bit easier. They know they can trust you. And so you give them a gift.

The Gift of Going Second.

It's the Gift of Going Second that starts waves of confession and healing.

I gave Crystal the Gift of Going Second when I shared my story of addiction with her. She found it a little bit easier to confess. But the gift doesn't stop there. Once you've experienced the power it has, you get to switch places and become the person who goes first for the people who have yet to confess.

You now get to give the Gift of Going Second.

Crystal took this responsibility and has given hundreds of women the Gift of Going Second. She went through some counseling and recovery and is getting healthier every day. Now, several years later, she's leading a "Victory over Sexual Sin" class for women at her church and has even started a ministry dedicated to helping women overcome pornography addiction.[22] She's had the chance to share her story from the stage at churches and online and for college students.

She keeps passing on the gift.

The Gift of Going Second.

25

EZRA'S CONFESSION

There's something about confession that is contagious and helps remove some of the fear associated with bringing something shameful and dark into the light.

I truly believe with all my heart that the world needs more people going first and giving the Gift of Going Second. If we can find the courage to confess something, even to just one person, the long-term effects of that confession can move others into rediscovering their faith and their freedom.

In the Old Testament, we meet a man named Ezra. He was a well-respected scribe and priest, known for his wisdom and having God's favor. The Bible says that God's favor wasn't on Ezra because of his knowledge; rather, he had committed his life to living the way God had instructed him—and he did so with his whole heart, his entire being. When it came to understanding, interpreting, and applying the law, some scholars consider Ezra the final authority in his particular culture.[23]

At first, Ezra lived in Babylon, and he received a request from the king to return to Jerusalem to help rebuild the temple. Before he began his journey, he prayed that God would protect him, along with the exiles and items they were carrying on their journey to Jerusalem.

They arrived in Jerusalem and took stock. Everything was in place. All the right people were there, and it appeared that everything was going fine. A few months in, Ezra discovered that the exiles in Jerusalem had started marrying into other tribes, which was against the law at the time.

Ezra was heartbroken that the people he was caring for had messed up. Even though he wasn't one of the people marrying outside of his tribe, the weight of the actions of his nation grieved him. He ripped his clothes and tore out some of his hair, which meant he saw himself just as guilty as everyone else.

When a group of people sinned like this, the guilt wasn't just on that person—the whole community was affected. When people saw Ezra responding to sin in the manner he was, they too began to grieve what had happened.

Ezra began to pray a very profound prayer of confession—out loud and very publicly:

> "My God, I am too ashamed and embarrassed to lift up my face to you, my God, because our sins are so many. They are higher than our heads. Our guilt even reaches up to the sky. From the days of our ancestors until now, our guilt has been great. Because of our sins, we, our kings, and our priests have been punished by the sword and captivity. Foreign kings have taken away our things and shamed us, even as it is today." Ezra 9:6–7

A few passages later, Scripture says that as Ezra was praying, broken on the ground, a group of Israelites surrounded him, agreeing and confessing with him. One man told him, "Get up, Ezra. You are in charge, and we will support you. Have courage and do it" (Ezra 10:4).

The responsibility the Israelites felt for one another, and their solidarity even in their brokenness is something we can learn from. Ezra, even though he was personally innocent, took a step and went first.

He gave the other Israelites the Gift of Going Second.

As I did with Crystal, Ezra took a deep breath and confessed. That one small action of speaking led to their personal and spiritual transformations. And those confessions didn't end there either. Many people who were trapped by shame have experienced the freedom that begins when somebody confesses.

After the Israelites confessed and began to heal, God did amazing things through them. The temple was rebuilt. It doesn't matter how much we have sinned, or what things we keep in the dark, or just how hidden we think we are from God—we may be out of His will, but we're not out of His reach. Remember how the father in the story of the lost son *ran* when he saw his son returning? Remember how he didn't require him to work his way back into the family? The same grace applies to us. And the Bible says the only thing we have to do is take a step into the light. When we respond like that, transformation will find its way into our hearts.

26

TO NEW YORK

My throat was burning from the cigarette smoke.

It wasn't my cigarette smoke. I haven't smoked since I was seven years old (once), but it was the smoke that had filtered into my New York City hotel room, causing my throat to feel like it was being attacked by fire-breathing dragons.

I tried sleeping with my head under the covers, as if that would somehow filter it, but that wasn't enough to stop it.

It was Saturday. The previous Tuesday, I booked a last-minute trip to New York City, home of the Empire State

Building, the world's most interesting cab rides, and my friend Jamie Tworkowski.

Jamie is the founder of an organization called To Write Love on Her Arms (TWLOHA). TWLOHA presents hope and finds help for people struggling with depression, addiction, self-injury, and suicide, and exists to encourage, inform, inspire, and also to invest directly into treatment and recovery.

Until three weeks before this manuscript was due to my publisher, I had no idea I'd be sharing his story, but in so many ways, it embodies the concept of the Gift of Going Second.

Jessica is Jamie's sister. She heard me speak at a conference once about the tension I've found when we talk about the messy and the beautiful. My thoughts on what and when and why and to whom I communicate the things I do in any forum have been shifting significantly over the last two years as I've been learning the value of speaking freely about the bad and the good.

I shared this in my session, and also how necessary it is to talk about whatever it is God is coming along and redeeming, no matter how uncomfortable or shameful or awkward the conversation might be, because there are other people who need to know they're not alone; for the health of our own souls we need to confess and live in community so we can be whole and healed.

After my talk, Jessica and her coworker Kaitlyn came up to the table where I was signing books and said they had attended my session and, after hearing me share, felt a kindred spirit.

One of the reasons TWLOHA exists is to help people realize they are not alone in their brokenness and to shine light into darkness. She really wished her brother Jamie had been in the session because we had so much in common, but since he wasn't, she insisted that I had to meet him. I *had* to.

I knew who Jamie was by reputation, although I'd never met him or heard him speak. I knew about To Write Love on Her Arms. I even had a few of their shirts. As a former graphic designer, I loved how they brought back the font Avant Garde. And if you don't love fonts as much as I do, I'm not sorry at all for admitting that. I love fonts.

Jamie was speaking right after me. I climbed up the stairs to the location of his presentation and took a seat on the floor of an overflowed room to hear him talk about To Write Love on Her Arms and the significance that comes when you surround yourself with people who will love you to hell and back.

If you're not familiar with To Write Love on Her Arms, let me share a little bit of their history with you. Then you'll be able to see why I was more than happy to book a last-minute trip to New York City to spend a few hours with Jamie and Jessica.

Renee Yohe was nineteen years old when Jamie met her. And the night they met, a combination of cocaine, pot, pills, and alcohol was coursing through her bloodstream. Her arms were scarred from trying to let her pain escape through the sharp edges of blades and glass. Jamie and his friends desperately wanted to take her to rehab, but she said no. Not that night. Maybe the next day.

She was tormented that night, haunted by the ghosts that had been following her for years—abuse, depression, and addiction—yet hope was holding on to a tender corner of her heart, pleading with her that her rescue was possible. Taking a razor blade and a drink, she wanted to quiet the voices again. She engraved a name in her arm—it's not her name, but it's how she identified herself.

"F*** Up."

Sometimes when people come across that word—the *F* word that is starred out in the sentence above—we think of it as profane.

Vulgar.

Inappropriate.

In this case, it's not.

Renee saw this word as her name. Her identity.

The following morning arrived, and Renee went to the rehab clinic. The nurse there turned her away. She was too much of a risk. Too many drugs were in her system; her wounds were too fresh.

"Come back later," the nurse said.

Over the next five days, Jamie and his friends became Renee's hospital. Her respite. Her place of healing. It's both tragic and beautiful. They immersed her in life and music and love.

The sunrises and sunsets mixed together, and a few days later it was time for her to go to treatment.

Jamie writes about those days:

We become her hospital and the possibility of healing fills our living room with life. It is unspoken and there are only a few of us, but we will be her church, the body of Christ coming alive to meet her needs, to write love on her arms. . . . I have watched life come back to her, and it has been a privilege. When our time with her began, someone suggested shifts, but that is the language of business. Love is something better. I have been challenged and changed, reminded that love is that simple answer to so many of our hardest questions. Don Miller says we're called to hold our hands against the wounds of a broken world, to stop the bleeding. I agree so greatly.

We often ask God to show up. We pray prayers of rescue. Perhaps God would ask us to be that rescue, to be His body, to move for things that matter. He is not invisible when we come alive. I might be simple, but more and more, I believe God works in love, speaks in love, is revealed in our love. I have seen that this week, and honestly, it has been simple: Take a broken girl, treat her like a famous princess, give her the best seats in the house. Buy her coffee and cigarettes for the coming down, books and bathroom things for the days ahead. Tell her something true when all she's known are lies. Tell her God loves her. Tell her about forgiveness, the possibility of freedom, tell her she was made to dance in white dresses. All these things are true.

We are only asked to love, to offer hope to the many hopeless. We don't get to choose all the endings, but we are

> asked to play the rescuers. We won't solve all mysteries, and our hearts will certainly break in such a vulnerable life, but it is the best way. We were made to be lovers bold in broken places, pouring ourselves out again and again until we're called home.
>
> I have learned so much in one week with one brave girl. She is alive now, in the patience and safety of rehab, covered in marks of madness but choosing to believe that God makes things new, that He meant hope and healing in the stars. She would ask you to remember.[24]

Jamie wrote an essay based on the five days he and his friends spent with Renee, so he could remember their sharp contrast of death and life and pain and hope. He created a MySpace page and posted the story and made some T-shirts to raise some money for treatment. Not long after, Jon Foreman, the lead singer of the band Switchfoot, wore the shirt at a concert in front of thousands of people who wondered what it meant. The message spread quickly.

But the movement didn't stop at the Switchfoot concert. TWLOHA provided a platform for other people to share. The Gift of Going Second never ends.

Through Renee's story, through her giving the Gift of Going Second, hundreds of thousands, maybe even millions of people have been able to speak freely, sometimes for the very first time. One person, Renee, went first, and it opened up a safe place for healing for so, so many others.

After learning about how Jamie shared Renee's story and how the movement of TWLOHA has set in motion so much healing, I knew this was an organization I needed to get to know better.

So I went to New York.

27

AN UNEXPECTED CAB CONFESSIONAL

Confession was already on my mind when I arrived in the torrential rains drenching the city. My flight got in after dark on Saturday night. Traveling alone in addition to the rainstorm caused me to reconsider my original plans to use public transportation. I decided to pay a little more for a cab instead of taking two trains and two subways to my hotel.

I've ridden in cabs in pretty much every major U.S. city (and internationally, for that matter) and each experience has been remarkable in some way. This trip was no exception. After hearing I looked like a movie star (it must have been my no-makeup face and airplane-frizzed hair), the driver asked if I was married.

"Yes. Six and a half years. To a very good, *very protective* man," I said, feeling slightly uneasy.

"That is a long time," he said. "You must get bored of him. Do you ever cheat?"

"No, I don't. . . . I love him. Are you married?"

"Yes. Three years. She just had a baby. We don't have the sex now. So I cheat on her with a customer. I am bored. I have no choice."

Oh. Expletive.

"You don't have a choice?"

"No. Men are different. We see a beautiful woman and we have to have the sex. Even if we watch the movie with a beautiful woman, it warms us up and we need to have the sex. I don't want to cheat, but I can't stop myself."

Oh. Expletive. Expletive.

"How long have you been driving a cab?" I asked, changing the subject and wondering if I jumped out of the cab if I could run to the nearest subway station without him chasing me.

"Five years. That is how I met the girlfriend. She knows I'm married, but she doesn't care. She's forty-two. I'm only twenty-nine. I like the older women. She says they are called cougars."

"I've heard that. How did you meet your wife?"

"It was arranged marriage."

"Do you love her?"

"Oh, very much. She is very beautiful. But I am bored."

"Does she know you cheat on her?"

"No," he laughed. "She would get very mad. So you never cheat. Your husband, does he cheat?"

"Pretty sure he doesn't."

"All men cheat. They just lie about it. They keep their actions the same so you don't know. Even priests."

"Really?"

"All the time."

I glanced around to see where we were.

Madison and Thirty-fourth.

We still had a long.

Way.

To.

Go.

I tried to redirect the conversation several times, but this guy had his mind set on one thing. Even though his confession was totally inappropriate and unprofessional and awkward, I didn't feel like I was in any real danger.

But more than that, I felt heartbroken for him.

I mean, after all, he said he didn't want to cheat.

He felt like he didn't have the strength to say no.

Somehow we got on the topic of smoking. He said he smoked. I asked him if he ever wanted to quit, and he said he had quit before. Sometimes for months, but he'd always go back. I told him that if he had enough willpower to stop smoking, maybe he was strong enough not to cheat, too, if he really didn't want to.

"I believe you can be strong," I told him.

He didn't believe me.

"The sex is different," he said.

And I know smoking and sex—sorry, "the sex"—are different. And ever since I stopped working in churches, I thought I was out of the Christian bubble. The truth of the matter is, those ninety minutes in a cab showed me how much I still live a very sheltered, very Southern, very bubbled life.

My cab driver was the world outside of my safe little sanctuary.

And on that Saturday night, his cab was a confessional.

My cab driver needed hope.

And faith.

And strength.

And truth.

He needed someone to carry the guilt he was feeling.

We arrived at my hotel. I gave him a nice tip and thanked him for driving me in the rain so safely. He told me I looked like a movie star again, and then he drove off, maybe to meet his cougar mistress.

Freedom doesn't discern whether you're comfortable or even if you believe in Jesus. It's a universal desire of our spirit, and this lovely and strange cab driver from Bangladesh showed me there's a world out there outside of the church that's searching for it.

From my hotel window, I stared out at the galaxy of city lights, feeling so very tiny yet so very determined to make every moment and every word count for love, regardless of where I am, who I'm with, or how uncomfortable it may be.

28

WE GET TO

I checked into my hotel and almost immediately went to bed, journaling about my cab ride and rolling the conversation over and over again in my head. I had been in New York for less than three hours, and already my heart had been sent into an unexpected state of awareness of humanity, and I hadn't even met with Jamie or Jessica yet.

The next morning I woke up and went from my smoky hotel room to the subway. A few stops later, I found myself in the east side of Manhattan, ringing the buzzer to Jamie's apartment. Jessica opened the door, and after a brief tour of Jamie's sublet (which included gravity boots hanging in the kitchen—Jamie swore they weren't his, but I have a feeling he's tried them out at least once or twice), the three of us headed to a café for breakfast so I could hear more about Jamie's journey and the profound effect To Write Love on Her Arms has had on so many people.

We eventually found a quiet café, and over coffee and breakfast, I asked why Jamie had even written about Renee.

"I know there are a lot of people who are involved with her story—of her getting clean and detoxing with you guys," I said, "but you've been the face of it to so many people. How do you tell someone else's story? Because first you have to earn her trust to tell it. What was that whole process like?"

He opened a packet of sugar and stirred it in his coffee, reflecting for a moment.

"You know," he said, "I would've understood if, when I asked her, 'Hey, what do you think about telling this story,' she said, 'Get lost.' But there was trust built in those few days. And in a way, it wasn't only her story—it was the story of the whole experience for all of us who were involved. When I wrote it, I didn't write it expecting tons of people to read it. I just wrote it for me, so I could remember the experience. I didn't expect for it to become the foundation of something so much bigger. And people have asked me to write a book about it, but that's not my place. Renee's a gifted storyteller. She can tell her own story. I was just the person to share a glimpse of it first. And now I get to share how her story is helping others."

I thought back to when I saw Jamie speak at the church leadership conference and wondered if he felt some of the same frustration with the church wanting to keep the appearance of everything being fine, when people are hurting around us.

"Absolutely. Sometimes my frustration with the church was like, hey, life is messy and it's everywhere. So why aren't we talking about it? If we avoid talking about brokenness, it's as if everything else is irrelevant. We need to deal with it. There are some statistics I share because they help paint a picture of that. In America, we've learned nineteen million people are depressed. And that untreated depression is also the leading cause of suicide. So when we find out that two out of three people who struggle with depression don't get help, that means a majority of people who live in that place live very much alone. I've heard it said so often that these things are born in secret and stay and grow in the dark. And that's really frightening."

A waitress interrupted us, bringing our food. I wondered if she heard us talking about depression and suicide. Jamie waited for her to leave and continued.

"It's easy to connect those dots between depression and suicide. And then the reality is that sometimes I'll share those things and say that I know they're not fun to hear about or talk about. But the good news is the conversation doesn't have to end there. Depression is very treatable. There's hope when people get help."

I took a bite of my yogurt and debated asking Jamie my

next question. I know that as I've had the chance to speak at places or write things, it's become really easy to talk about something but not practice it. I remember a few months after my book on health released, I was about to go out for a few weeks to talk about it. One night I woke up in a sweaty panic. I hadn't been eating right because I was stressed, and I had been living in a cycle of sleeping pills at night and espresso shots in the morning. I hadn't talked to anyone about how stressed I was, and here I was, supposedly the poster child for health. Jamie talked a lot about living in community with others and sharing where we're really hurting the most, but I wondered if he lived it out. I figured I'd be bold and went for the kill.

"So Renee's story has become part of your story. And because it's all about living transparently with people, do you ever have a hard time actually living that out?" I took another bite of yogurt and wondered if he'd either punch me in the face for asking him such a personal question or if he'd give me a Christian pat answer. He did neither.

He waited a moment, and I could tell he was gathering his thoughts. He wrapped both his hands around the Styrofoam cup in front of him and took a drink before responding.

"Yeah. I mean, that's in some ways the reason I'm here in New York. It's gotten to a point where speaking from the stage is kind of easy, you know. The stage is a privilege, and I believe in the stuff I'm saying, but to live out the relational side of it is totally difficult. Here I am, talking about living in relationships with people, and I started to realize that I don't have any of the stuff I'm talking about. When I'd go home to where I grew up in Florida, I'd feel totally bankrupt. So that's why I moved to New York. I have more solid relationships here. It's been a season of choosing friends, but also of choosing to get help where I need it. I went back to counseling and I started on antidepressants for the first time. And I feel like I can talk about this stuff now."

That was not the answer I was expecting at all. I sat back a little bit in awe that Jamie had so freely shared that his life for the last couple of years had been difficult. That he had been talking about people getting help for depression and he was depressed. And he started to get help. He was speaking out of a place where he was truly living.

He continued, "It's like I'm able to say it's okay. That people deal with this and that I deal with this. And it's been added to my story. I can speak on it because I'm living it. There are real steps you can take to get help, and we really aren't meant to live life alone. We just have to share it with someone. It may be getting coffee with a friend or maybe it's counseling or maybe it's both. It's been cool to see how it resonated with so many people, because people really do think they're alone. And they're not."

"You know," I said, "that's kind of the same reason Chris and I moved to Nashville. We had been jumping all around—Kansas . . . Texas . . . Oklahoma . . . and then Nashville. But we noticed how much time we'd spend in Nashville when we didn't live there and the depth of the relationships we had there. We kept asking ourselves why we didn't move there, and finally a friend said, 'Why be miserable? Move!' and we did. And it takes time and intentionality, but we're really connecting with people. It feels like home."

"I like Nashville," Jamie said. He looked around for another packet of sugar for his coffee. As he tore open the packet, he went back to talking about relationships.

"It's funny; I feel I end up being a bit of a broken record because I keep saying it's about community, or whatever you want to call it. We just need honest relationships. But for a lot of people, that's a scary place to start. But the burden of fearing those relationships is so much heavier than actually having them. Once we have them, we realize how necessary they are."

I took another bite of my breakfast and agreed with him. "It's been totally scary talking to people about my own depression. Even just the other day I was having dinner with a friend of mine named Kyle. Somehow we got on the topic of depression, and I shared with Kyle what the last few seasons have looked like. I kind of threw all these emotions up on him that I had been stuffing, and after I was done, I apologized. Kyle asked me why I was apologizing, and I told him it was because I didn't want to burden him with all that—he didn't need to carry it around. And you know what he said to me? He said, 'Anne, when you tell me these things, it's okay. First, I'm another Christian, and that's what we're supposed to do, right? Doesn't Galatians 6 talk about that? Anyway, I'm really not even carrying it. I'm carried by the grace of Christ, and so that's how it all gets carried in the end. That's how we're able to carry these burdens for one another. That's why they're not too heavy to carry."

Something I said about mine and Kyle's conversation sparked something in Jamie. His eyes lit up.

"Okay," he said, tugging on the sleeves of his jacket and leaning forward on the table. "I'm sort of a freak about Bono. So there's this song U2 does called 'One,' and there's a line in it that says, 'We get to carry each other.' I read an interview recently where Bono talked about how it makes him mad when people sing that line wrong. They sing 'We *have* to carry each other' instead of 'We *get* to carry each other.' So basically, he said if you sing it like we *have* to carry each other, we're missing the privilege of it. We don't have to—we *get* to. It's an obligation, and stretch, and it takes so much effort. But in the end, it's a privilege that we *get* to carry each other. That's just so right on. It's so true."

We chatted a little more about some practical things TWLOHA does with the awareness and the funds they raise, and we began to leave the café. It was Jessica's first time to visit her brother in the city, and he wanted to take us around his neighborhood and show us some stuff, like Washington Square Park and a bar where Jeff Buckley used to play. Jessica had remained pretty quiet during our breakfast, but as we were leaving, she summed up the Gift of Going Second so beautifully.

"There's such a need for people to be able to talk about all of these things. So we've just tried to create an environment where we say it's not only okay to share this stuff; it's essential. And I think that's it. We've seen this incredible response because it's like bringing water to the desert. People come up to us so many times—I can't tell you how many times—and simply say, 'Thank you for talking about this,' which, in a way, is them saying, 'Thank you for inviting me to talk about this. You mentioned it first, so now I can."

Jamie held open the door as we walked onto Fourteenth Street.

"It's like giving them the permission to go second," I said.

"Exactly."

We spent the next few hours meandering the streets of New York, talking about music and dog parks and history, and Jamie took us to try some crab pizza from a hole-in-the-wall spot off Second Avenue. I typically don't like crab, but it was ridiculously good.

Outside of Jamie's apartment, I hailed a cab and wondered if this driver would confess something to me like my first cab driver did. He didn't say a word to me, and instead spoke in Hindi to someone on the other side of his Bluetooth the entire twenty-five minutes to the airport.

We all have our secrets, and we all want to be rescued. I couldn't help but wonder what this cab driver was holding close. I wondered if he was one of the nineteen million Americans who were depressed. I wondered if someone was carrying him.

Because we all need to be carried at some point. Even cab drivers from Bangladesh or thirty-year-olds who find themselves in the limelight of a movement.

We all need to be carried, and we all get to carry.

And it's grace that holds us up so we don't collapse under the weight of it all.

Amazing Grace

Amazing grace! (how sweet the sound)
That sav'd a wretch like me!
I once was lost, but now am found,
Was blind, but now I see.

'Twas grace that taught my heart to fear,
And grace my fears reliev'd;
How precious did that grace appear,
The hour I first believ'd!

Thro' many dangers, toils and snares,
I have already come;
'Tis grace has brought me safe thus far,
And grace will lead me home.

The Lord has promis'd good to me,
His word my hope secures;
He will my shield and portion be,
As long as life endures.

Yes, when this flesh and heart shall fail,
And mortal life shall cease;
I shall possess, within the veil,
A life of joy and peace.

The earth shall soon dissolve like snow,
The sun forbear to shine;
But God, who call'd me here below,
Will be forever mine. [25]

29

SEVEN STEPS

This is the way a book sometimes comes together:

AUTHOR CHECKLIST FOR TYPICAL BOOK WRITING

- ☑ Share some stories and illustrations about your life. (Check.)
- ☑ If writing from a Christian point of view, share stories and illustrations from the Bible and about the church. (Check.)
- ☑ People are voyeuristic by nature, so they like to read about other people. Share other people's stories. (Check.)
- ☐ End the book with seven steps of practical advice on how to accomplish whatever goal you have in mind for them.

If you haven't noticed by now, this isn't structured like a self-help book. In fact, if you are reading this chapter, that means my editor and I have arm-wrestled and I won and we got to break the rules of the typical book structure.

And you've made it to the end.

You've challenged yourself to think outside chapters that seamlessly flow in and out of each other and instead jumped into a messy combination of art and story and Scripture.

Thank you.

I wrote a book one time that was full of practical advice. There were five principles of staying healthy in four specific areas of health. It had an outline. It was easy to write, as far as books go. But whenever I would talk about the book or have people ask me questions about the book, I began to realize that most of the time, people's lives didn't match the five principles or the four areas, and while the road map was helpful for many people, it didn't really solve the world's problems or anything.

And so I began to wonder. Can a book actually change the world?

My gut feeling? No. Books can't. But people can.

I'll admit. It's been challenging to write this book. I had a vague outline that existed only to keep me from writing too much about my cat (which still may have happened). As I wrote, and the manuscript changed (morphed into an unrecognizable life-form is a truer statement), I got more and more nervous. It seemed as if every book I had read in the last ten years had a great flow, a great outline, and resolved tension. As I got deeper and deeper into my manuscript, I felt more unresolved tension.

Crap.

Over sushi one night (I like saying *sushi* because it makes me sound trendy when, in fact, I don't eat sushi and only had soup), two writer friends of mine, Susan and Shelia, talked about story and resolution. I laid out my dilemma to them.

"My book doesn't have an ending. It doesn't tell people what to do next."

They consoled me and told me it was okay.

"But people don't buy books that don't tell them what to do."

They assured me that was not my problem, and instead the problem is the people who don't buy books that don't have easy answers.

Of course they would say that.

This isn't their book.

A few days after our sushi and/or soup, Shelia wrote an essay based on our conversation. It's about choosing art that challenges you.

Art that doesn't spoon-feed you the answers.

I thought her essay was lovely, and I asked her if I could share it with you.

> As we grow up, we learn a great deal about the mysteries that perplexed us when we were small. We learn that the sun doesn't go to bed after all. Our earth just turns away

from her for a bit. The stars that look like diamonds sparkling in the sky are really nasty balls of flaming gas. And bit by bit, we surrender the magic that was once our constant companion.

We come to believe that truth must be quantifiable and verifiable. "Just the facts, ma'am." We even want our stories (and our faith) tied up in neat little bows with simplistic morals and clearly defined good guys and bad guys. But that is not life. And that is not truth. Life and truth are far more complex, and messy, and rich, and wonderful. But they require a good deal of work.

Jesus did the same thing. Why did he respond to questions with questions? Why did he tell stories? Because he knew the truest things in life must be discovered . . . through wrestling . . . through blood and sweat and tears.

I understand that sometimes we use movies or books to escape. We want something simple. A place to rest. But I encourage you to sometimes choose art that challenges you . . . art that can take you places you can't get to by yourself. Read Dostoevsky or Chesterton. Listen to Rachmaninoff or Philip Glass. Watch *Crash*, or *Big Fish*, or anything by Wes Anderson. Stand in front of art created in the last hundred years. Discover the poetry of Rilke, Berry, or Merton. Bring your dreams and your imagination with you.

And wrestle.[26]

With that said, I hope the stories and art and poetry in this book have been challenging, and instead of ending it with four chapters that give you step-by-step instructions on how to be free from fear for the rest of your life, or tell you how to confess, I am going to let it be.

Here's the thing. You have to do your part, and only you will know what that looks like in your life at this moment. Maybe you'll read this book again in one year or three years, and that will look different to you than it does now.

But the only point is that you have a story. And this story is made up of your past and present and future, and many things color it. People who have hurt you, the church that hurt you, the challenges you've beat to a bloody pulp, things you've done that you're not proud of, and the beauty that's in every breath—each breath that's filled with regret and each breath that's filled with life.

With all of these things comes an amazing opportunity to step up and confess—not only the bad, but confess the good and noble as well.

Yes, the world is beautifully broken, and it wraps us up in both extremes. But in the end, our story comes back to us. Humanity is wonderful and flawed because I am wonderful and flawed. Humanity is wonderful and flawed because you are wonderful and flawed. And when we confess the simple truth of both to each other, we embrace the grace and mercy our Father God has given us.

Then somehow all those broken pieces come together in an awkward mosaic and we find life.

We find healing.

We find hope.

Yes, we have been broken. Sometimes we've been broken a lot. Some of us think we've done too much, or had so much done to us that we're not worth being rescued. Please believe me when I say each and every one of us is being rescued. It's a precarious and unpredictable path, but taking it is worth every shaky, uncertain step.

The one, solid, faithful promise of truth in all of this is that we are being rescued.

And it's time for you to tell someone about it.

It's time for you to speak freely.

Is it scary? Absolutely.

But on the other side of any fear you may have there is a freedom beyond anything you can possibly comprehend. And, you see, once you move beyond your fear into confession and transformation, your voice and your actions can take you one step further away from fear.

Each time we decide to take a step away from fear, we begin to move forward into a life completely energized and rich in the freedom God has for us. And as we take more steps into freedom, our actions have the power to set others on that same course of freedom as well.

Only you can give yourself permission.

Not me. Not this book.

Not the church, whether you go to one or not.

Only you can give yourself the permission to speak freely.

Don't let fear stop you.

Somebody is waiting on you to tell your story. To share how you're being rescued. To share how scary it is but how beautiful it is. Someone is waiting for the little ounce of courage that your voice can give them, so they can begin to find their own piece of freedom.

And even beyond that, somebody is waiting on *that* person.

It all can really begin with you.

So take a step.

Confess the beautiful and broken.

It happens one word at a time.

I don't think on this side of heaven you'll ever become completely fearless—but you can act courageously in spite of that fear. So speak.

Freely.

The world needs you to.

ACKNOWLEDGMENTS

If every person who deserved a thank-you was listed in this book, it would easily double the size of it, and with the industry the way it is, I don't think my publisher, as kind as they are, would want to use another couple hundred pages of paper.

Sometimes I feel like each person who has crossed my path is one thread of many who have been woven in and out and in between others, and those threads are what make up the fiber of who I am. Some threads are short, others are still being sewn in, some are silky and smooth, while others are coarse and colorful, but they have one thing in common: they hold me together. So if our souls have ever crossed paths, I sincerely thank you.

I'd like to lavish gratitude on my husband, Chris, for reading this manuscript several thousand times in all of its various stages and sacrificing the big dreams we had planned for a much smaller but much more meaningful dream. He also does the dishes, which is the key to my heart.

To my friends "on campus," so much of this book has been written between meals and long talks on porches with you. Those things feed my soul and inspire me to trust again, one conversation at a time. You have been family to us. Thank you for loving me on my artist days when I haven't showered.

Geography doesn't limit the love I have for several people who have shown me unconditional and consistent support through an interesting year of transition: Crystal Renaud, Lynse Stevens, Kyle and Holiday Zimmerman, L. V. Hanson, Ben Arment, Mike Foster, Jud Wilhite, Brad Lomenick, Ian Cron, Seth Godin, Dino and DeLynn Rizzo, Perry and Lucretia Noble, Charlie Neese and Eve Annunziato, Donald Miller, Susan Isaacs, Christine Caine, Len and Elizabeth Sweet, Annie Downs, Sheila Walsh, Mary Graham, Patsy Clairmont, Ryan O'Neal, Jamie Tworkowski, Jessica Haley, Shaun Groves, Chad Davis, Brandon Holt (and Paul) at Chadwick's Fitness, St. Bartholomew's, Healing Place Church, The Oaks, Cross Point Church, Faith Promise Church, NewSpring Church, Jars of Clay, and the lovely people at Catalyst.

The people who surround me professionally care more

about the right thing than the bottom line: Beth Jusino (I miss you!), Rick Christian and Andrea Heiencke, Angela Scheff, Ryan Pazdur, Brad Ruggles, Joe Gomez, Lee Steffen, Jim Chaffee, and Michele Bennett. Also my incredible team at Thomas Nelson: Mike Hyatt, Matt Baugher, Jennifer McNeil, Jennifer Stair, Dale Wilstermann, Emily Sweeney, Kristi Johnson, Stephanie Newton, the dazzling sales team who are too numerous and too dazzling to mention individually, and everyone else who has touched this manuscript in some way.

These organizations are close to my heart: Compassion International, To Write Love on Her Arms, Blood:Water Mission/Ride:Well Tour, Dirty Girls Ministries, People of the Second Chance, the Mentoring Project, and XXXchurch.com. You should see if they can be close to yours too.

Almost there . . . (deep breath!). Thank you to my family and the people in my past who have shaped me into the person I am becoming. The best and the worst moments of the last thirty years could never have been predicted, and I wouldn't go back to change a single thing. I hope to continue cultivating love, gratitude, kindness, forgiveness, and above all, truth.

And thank you, of course, for allowing me to share a piece of my heart and my story with you.

NOTES

1. Anne Jackson, "Tension," date unknown.
2. Anne Jackson, "trust is not a four-letter word," date unknown.
3. Anne Jackson, "What's Done Is Done," 1996/1997.
4. Anne Jackson, "Lady Trust," date unknown.
5. It was an encouragement to me to see individuals and organizations that were connected to this man, standing up for the right thing. They entered the due diligence process, investigating the situation, bringing in experts and authorities, confronting him, and providing the necessary corrective paths. Their actions gave me a sense of protection and justice in a time in which I had questioned the existence of these qualities.
6. Sleeping at Last, "Naive," used with permission by author, Ryan O'Neal.

7. *New York Times*, 1880, public domain.
8. Norman MacLaren Trenholme, *The Right of Sanctuary in England: A Study in Institutional History* (University of Missouri, 1903), public domain.
9. Scott Walker Hahn, *Lord, Have Mercy* (New York: Doubleday, 2003).
10. *Adam and Eve Hiding*, Woodcut—N. Pisana, Orvieto. *The History of Our Lord as Exemplified in Works of Art*, vol. 1. (London: Longmans, Green & Co., 1872), public domain.
11. Matthew Henry, *Complete Commentary on Genesis 3*, public domain.
12. *The Lord Accusing Adam and Eve.* "Bible de Noailles"—AD 1000, Bibliotheque Royale, Paris. *The History of Our Lord as Exemplified in Works of Art*, vol. 1.
13. Hahn, *Lord, Have Mercy*, 16.
14. Paraphrased from Rob Bell in a sermon titled "Confession," Mars Hill Church, Grandville, MI, July 18, 2009.
15. Tim Keller, *The Prodigal God* (New York: Dutton Adult, 2008).
16. Ibid., 78.
17. Anne Jackson, "Found," date unknown.
18. Thank you to Dr. Andrew Pickett at St. Thomas Heart in Nashville for diagnosing and curing my heart arrhythmia.
19. Anne Jackson, "The Rescue," 2009.
20. Three Way Stop, "Silence," used with permission.
21. Jon Acuff is the author of *Stuff Christians Like* (Grand Rapids: Zondervan, 2010), and a good friend.
22. Dirty Girls Ministries, http://www.dirtygirlsministries.com.
23. F. Charles Fensham, *The Books of Ezra and Nehemiah, The New International Commentary on the Old Testament* (Grand Rapids: Eerdmans, 1982).
24. Jamie Tworkowski, To Write Love on Her Arms, twloha.com, 2006.
25. Amazing Grace, John Newton, 1779.
26. Shelia Mullican, http://anam-cara.typepad.com, October 20, 2009. Used with permission.

To request Anne Jackson to speak at your church or organization, visit www.chaffeemanagement.com or call 615.236.1682.

Get Connected!

Twitter:
www.twitter.com/flowerdust

Facebook:
www.facebook.com/flowerdust

Blog:
www.flowerdust.net

Book site:
www.permissiontospeakfreely.com

MAKE YOUR OWN CONFESSION

How can you be a part of the movement to Speak Freely? Easy!

1) Write down your confession. What's something you feel like you can't say in church? You can make it as short or as long as you want. You can write it on anything you want—a piece of paper, like a letter, a postcard, a bulletin, a page from the Bible, a photograph, a drawing, *anything* at all that you can mail. It can be any shape, any size. It doesn't have to be super creative (although it certainly can be). It can just be something written down. You also don't have to currently attend church or even believe in God.

2) Put at LEAST your first name on it. This is a revolution to claim our brokenness and God's redemption. You can use your full name if you want, but your first name is fine.

3) Stick a stamp on it and mail it in. Send it to Permission to Speak Freely, PO Box 431, Franklin, TN 37065. Or if you're a fancy Photoshopper, make it a digital file that is at least 300dpi at 6" x 4" and e-mail it to speak@permissiontospeakfreely.com

Your confession may be posted online at www.permissiontospeakfreely.com.*

** By submitting information to this project, you grant Anne Jackson a perpetual, royalty-free license to use, reproduce, modify, publish, distribute, and otherwise exercise all copyright and publicity rights with respect to that information at its sole discretion, including storing it on her servers and incorporating it in other works in any media now known or later developed, including without limitation published books. If you do not wish to grant her these rights, it is suggested that you do not submit information. Anne Jackson/Thomas Nelson reserves the right to select, edit, and arrange submissions, and to remove information from the website at any time at its sole discretion*